THE DINNER PARTY

9 MENUS 107 RECIPES FOREVER MEMORIES BY MARTIN BENN & VICKI WILD PHOTOGRAPHY KRISTOFFER PAULSEN

THIS BOOK IS DEDICATED TO THOSE WHO GIVE US SO MUCH TO TALK ABOUT AT DINNER PARTIES!

Hardie Grant

BOOKS

THE START
6

THE MENUS

THE COCKTAILS 208

THE BASICS 212

W

WE MUST DO THIS MORE OFTEN

e're having a dinner party. Those few words can either cue meltdown, anxiety and uncertainty ... or anticipation, excitement and joy.

This book comes from a deep desire to see people coming together to eat, drink and have fun in their own homes, with their own food on the table.

As a chef and restaurateur, I have cooked and entertained my whole life, always striving to create a meal that will never be forgotten. As much as I love casual get-togethers and bring-a-plate suppers, there is a very special thrill that comes from planning and preparing something extraordinary.

People get it. They get that you are doing this for them because you value their friendship or their company. Otherwise, why would you bother? Entertaining is an act of generosity. You are giving your time and your energy to making people feel intrigued, delighted, contented.

But I'm not going to pretend it's a walk in the park. Being organised is the sword by which you live and die here. If you're the type to leave everything to the last minute and then throw it all together, may I gently suggest you support the hospitality industry and book a restaurant instead.

THERE ARE NO RULES ANYMORE

In the past, entertaining at home was very formal, as carefully set out as the dazzling array of cutlery on the table. There were rules of play, and strict etiquette to follow. Then followed, in Australia at least, a wonderful sense of freedom, in which we embraced our more casual nature and our love of the great outdoors. By the 1970s, the barbecue was the high point on the entertaining calendar, as the men hovered over the coals at one end of the backyard and the women tossed salads in the kitchen.

Then, for the last two or three years, we couldn't get together. We Zoomed over cocktails and FaceTimed over dinner, but it just wasn't the same. People need people in order to bring out the best in themselves. My partner-in-crime Vicki Wild and I couldn't wait to start entertaining again.

We dreamed about it, devising fantasy guest lists and visualising our dining table covered in glorious food. We swore to each other that when we could entertain again, we would do it with all the bells and whistles, with all our hearts. And without any rules.

A dinner party doesn't have to be formal, and nor does it have to be casual. What it does have to be is an expression of you, the host. You must bring to it your character and personality, your humour and your skills.

Me? I bring truffles. Ever since the French Périgord truffle variety was introduced into Tasmania twenty years ago, I have tried to celebrate their short, precious season in every way possible.

For some people, a football grand final or a great musician's concert is a special time. For me, it's truffle season. Every year, I have planned a great truffle dinner so I can share my obsession with friends.

From those annual dinners came the idea to celebrate the dinner party in all its glory. Not just to create a feast of seasonal foods, but to elevate dining and make it special again.

LET'S TALK ABOUT THE FOOD

Australia's food identity and evolution over the past fifty years has shaped us into one of the great food destinations of the world. Our dinner parties should reflect that. We don't need to slavishly follow the rules of another country or culture, but rather, we should make our own way, write our own story, cook our own food.

Our unique Indigenous ingredients are one way of telling our story and acknowledging and respecting the First Peoples of this land. But we each bring a multitude of cultural influences to the table, and together, make Australia what it is.

My story, as a bricklayer's son brought up in south-eastern England who discovered the world through cooking, and who fell in love with the subtlety and power of Japanese cuisine, is now an Australian story, too.

And so, we all shape an Australian cuisine, together. In the past, the ideas in this book would have been sniffily described as 'fusion' cooking. That time is long behind us.

Come to dinner. The evening might start with prawn toasts with sansho and sesame, and go on to blackened piri-piri chicken. The salad might be heirloom tomatoes with toasted garlic oil and shichimi togarashi; the dessert a caramelised apple and miso butterscotch semifreddo. (And if that appeals, go directly to Menu 6 on page 125!). I don't call that fusion. I call it fused.

We have fused who we are, and where we are, into something very exciting.

WE MUST DO THIS MORE OFTEN

The Dinner Party is based on actual dinner parties held at our home. The themes, the dishes, the wines and the playlists all actually happened. We threw ourselves into the tasks of shopping, chopping, prepping, cooking, serving and cleaning up.

We love gathering in the kitchen as guests arrive; the tinkle of ice in a cocktail shaker; the crisp bite of a hot pastry. Then the move to the table, the wine, the music, the flowers, the careful choosing of delicate platters and bowls. As host, you build the magic like a stage manager, setting a scene in which people can relax, and also be excited by what is to come.

And you know what? It worked. Because every single time, somebody would look around and smile, and say 'We must do this more often.' Hopefully, with this book as inspiration, we all will.

MAKE IT FUN

To theme or not to theme? A theme can start with the simplest thing – the time of year, a colour, or a feeling. It can be inspired by an ingredient such as a great cut of meat, a fresh haul of seafood or a highly seasonal mushroom. Some of our finest dinner parties have been inspired by a bottle of wine.

In fact, we are blessed with a number of wine-loving, cellar-owning friends, and when one of them suggests getting together over dinner in order to celebrate a special vintage or a rare varietal, we jump at the chance.

Like many good things, this all started with a bunch of close friends who love food and wine. We'd meet at the home of the legendary wine writer Huon Hooke, who would create a theme of sorts. We'd all bring a dish, Huon would open bottle after bottle, and we'd all have so much fun.

Dinner parties aren't about showing off, they're about sharing, about setting the scene for good times. Creating a theme for each occasion not only makes each dinner party completely different, it also makes life easier, narrowing down the options.

Themes can also be unspoken; just something you work towards without necessarily sharing with your guests. Something for your own amusement.

THE ALL-IMPORTANT GUESTS

Guests are just as much ingredients of a great dinner party as those in the kitchen. And in the same way, they come waiting to be transformed, uplifted, into something special.

The very best number of people to invite, depending on your table, is six; any more and the conversation tends to split. With six, you can talk together, hear each other, speak to those either side of you and across the table. A good mix of couples and singles makes it lively. And while there's nothing better than meeting up with old friends, we often invite people who have never met, which makes it more interesting for everyone.

PLANNING THE MENU

As you may have gathered, my mantra is to make it fun. And planning the menu is the most fun part of the whole process.

Start with one main ingredient and build the menu from there. Always check that your guests are able and willing to eat everything, and don't worry too much if there are a couple of requests to avoid certain things – that can actually help you narrow the number of options.

Martin will always take that into account and cook dishes that everyone can share, so that those with any dietary issues aren't made to feel different. It's all part of making people feel welcome and looked after.

There's nothing wrong with the old-school entrée, main course, dessert format, but for a dinner party, it's more dynamic to have quite a few small dishes, some individually plated and some shared. That way, small eaters can take what they like (and so can large eaters!), and don't have to worry about leaving food on their plate.

COCKTAILS AND CANAPÉS

People can be a little nervous when they come to your home for the first time, so do what you can to help them relax. We love gathering around the kitchen bench and opening a bottle of Champagne. It's festive and celebratory, and it lets people know you value their company. A big bowl of olives on the bench is a nice touch for those who arrive hungry.

Cocktails and canapés are great icebreakers; there is nothing better than a classic cocktail, done well. These days, there are some great, considered options for non-drinkers as well. That doesn't often happen at our place, but when it does, we put just as much thought and care into the making of an alcohol-free cocktail as we do any other.

Always have plenty of water, and make it easy for guests to keep their glasses topped up. We carbonate our own because we like a sparkle, and it's much more cost-effective and better for the environment than buying imported water.

THERE ARE NO RULES

Another mantra, and a good one. Who says, for instance, that you have to serve dessert? Sometimes we finish by putting out some beautiful cheeses and accompaniments. In winter, we warm a whole cheese in the oven and serve it like fondue – very decadent.

Mind you, it never ceases to amaze me how many people will announce they couldn't possibly eat another thing, but then out comes a spectacular dessert (and Martin's are truly spectacular!) and it disappears in no time flat.

If you do dessert, have it already prepared so all that is needed is a finishing touch when it's time to serve. And if you haven't been able to achieve that, sometimes just a bowl of bittersweet chocolate or Italian biscotti can make a beautiful finale.

MUSIC TO OUR EARS

Our background in restaurants has given us great insight into the role music can play in setting a mood and dialling the energy up or down. That's why we always make a playlist of different tracks that we think will suit the occasion.

Even though the two of us have very different taste in music, we come together over a shared love of jazz, so that's always on the agenda. As you'll see, the playlists offered for each menu are deliberately very eclectic. And I haven't had a dinner party yet where someone hasn't turned their favourite track way up high! (Okay, that might have been me.)

DONT BE SWEATING THE TABLE SETTING

I love a beautiful table, but that doesn't mean fancy and formal. The best tables are simple and welcoming. Glasses gleam, napkins are cloth, and there's a little greenery from the garden or some small flowers arranged in with the candles.

After years of running fine-dining restaurants, I have a fetish for crockery and cutlery, and have collected some stunning things, both high and low, expensive and streetwise. That's the thing: not everything has to be perfect, or matchy-matchy. I love a bit of a mix of cutlery and napkins, and choose bowls and plates that I feel will show off the food to its best advantage.

Having the table set when guests arrive is a nice touch, and leaves you with little to do. If nothing else, just dim the lights and set out some candles, and everyone will relax and enjoy themselves. It's your home, and it should feel that way to you and your guests.

RELAX, IT'S ONLY DINNER

Repeat after me: make it fun. You've done all the planning and cooking, so make sure you relax and let your hair down. There is nothing more pleasurable in life than good food, good wine, good friends and good conversation. The added bonus is that remarkable, memorable and exciting things can come out of a dinner party. It's like a team bonding exercise, with guards let down, friendships deepened and experiences shared. (Although what happens at the dinner party stays at the dinner party, right?)

Here's to a lifetime of dinner parties, and the dinner parties of a lifetime!

HOW TO USE THIS BOOK

This is not just a book of recipes, it's a book of dreams. As you turn the pages, allow yourself to imagine your guests turning up at the door, the first dishes coming to the table, the smiles and excited chatter.

CHOOSE A MENU

If one of the menus stops you in your tracks, engage with it. Run your eye down the dishes, and check out the photographs so you know what you're aiming for.

Each recipe is designed to serve six people, but don't feel you have to make every dish in your chosen menu. This isn't some form of endurance test, it's just a few ideas for how to achieve dinner party nirvana. Choose the recipes that appeal to you the most and that you feel you can achieve without stress.

As a guide, a classic dinner party would go something like this:

ONE OR TWO CANAPÉS OR SNACKS, READY TO GO

**ONE OR TWO ENTRÉES,
SHARED OR INDIVIDUALLY PLATED**

PASTA OR NOODLE DISH

**MAIN COURSE,
WITH A POTATO OR RICE DISH ON THE SIDE**

VEGETABLE SIDE DISH OR SALAD

DESSERT, OF COURSE, OR CHEESE

READ IT THROUGH

In each recipe, I give a breakdown of what to prep and cook, and when. I genuinely believe that to get the best end result – for both the food and for you, the cook – you need to think a couple of days ahead.

These stages start with Prep Ahead, and go on to From the Pantry, Day Before and On the Day. They are there to help you plan your time, with further explanation in the actual recipe method.

PREP AHEAD

Just two words, but what a difference they make. Any chef knows that without mise en place, they're dead in the water. Mise en place simply means 'to put in place': to have everything you need ready to go.

Knowing what you can prepare two days ahead, or the day before, is really helpful, and so is knowing how to store the food you have prepared.

There's not much point throwing delicate greens into the fridge unwrapped, or leaving seafood to sit in its own juices instead of on absorbent paper towel. Look after your food at this stage and it will reward you by retaining freshness and texture until the moment you serve it.

Some components actually improve by being prepared ahead of time, such as sauces and dressings, and even braised meats. Stored in the coldest part of the refrigerator in their own braising liquid, their flavour deepens so much more than it would had you braised them on the day.

FROM THE PANTRY

If an item is listed under From the Pantry, the recipe for it will be in the Basics chapter. Some of these sauces, dressings, oils and butters can be made weeks or even months in advance. They're a cook's best friends, there when you need them.

For example, I find myself making chicken stock once every four weeks, and shellfish oil once every three months. It stops me getting anxious about getting low on something. This is vital not just for dinner parties, but for adding extra oomph to a midweek dinner, too. Get into the habit of using your pantry staples often and replacing them often; that keeps them in rotation and keeps them fresh.

DAY BEFORE

These are the things you can do a day ahead, and store in a way that protects them from spoilage, without compromising their integrity.

ON THE DAY

These are the things that require freshness and immediacy and must be cooked to order; that need to be done on the day of serving. If a recipe has multiple stages, I will suggest what can be done in the morning, and what is best left until the afternoon.

All your herbs or garnishes, such as sliced cucumbers or diced radishes, for example, can be prepared in the morning, leaving the afternoon for things like searing fish or meat in the hour prior to guests coming.

LESS IS MORE

The less you have to do on the night, the more time you can spend with your guests. I know where I would rather be.

EQUIPMENT

Having the right equipment makes everything easier.

Here's a list of everything used to create and test the recipes in this book. I deliberately avoided high-tech professional equipment, and used what was in my own cupboards and kitchen drawers.

You won't necessarily have everything listed here, of course, but this is a great guide to a well set-up kitchen that you can work towards establishing over time. And once you have the right tools, you will use them again and again.

In my home kitchen, I am just as organised as in a restaurant kitchen, because I don't like having to root around trying to find the item I need for a particular task. The tools I use often are kept close by, and those I use rarely, and the more specialised pastry and dessert tools, are stored in separate areas.

Another big tip is to reduce the clutter by not having too many duplicates. We all keep old, damaged or worn favourites, even after buying new, improved ones. Bite the bullet: remove the old, and move on.

THE JOY OF CONTAINERS

You can never have enough containers. Or at least, I never can. Something inside me dies when I see food stored incorrectly for lack of the right container.

Having a good selection of containers means perishable foods will last longer, liquids will not spill, and your refrigerator will not be full of strange, competing odours. Some foods, such as eggs, are pervious, allowing the aroma of other food items, such as garlic, to permeate them. For that reason, eggs are best kept in a sealed container rather than in the egg holders in the door of your refrigerator.

Develop your own system for storage and you will find things more easily, and extend the life of your food. Buy the right size containers to fit into your freezer or pantry, and make sure they stack neatly. Small containers are great for spices, and large ones are perfect for salad leaves and braised meats, for example. The most useful size is 1 litre (34 fl oz), for general usage. Label the containers and you'll be able to see what you have at a glance.

ESSENTIALS

blowtorch

Champagne stopper, wine stopper

cheese slicer, single blade

chopping boards, various

corkscrew

kitchen fish pliers

knives: chef knife (large and medium), paring knife, fish slicing knife, serrated knife, bread knife, tomato knife (small, serrated), sharpening steel, finger palette knife, step palette knife (medium and large), fish spatula, wide-step palette knife

ladles, various

lemon squeezer

meat tenderiser

metal pouring jugs

Microplane graters, from fine to coarse

mortar and pestle

oil pourer for bottles

olive pitter

pasta colander

pencil thermometer

roasting fork

salad spinner

slotted spoon

spider (webbed ladle)

tongs, various

truffle slicer

vegetable peeler

wooden spoons

PASTRY EQUIPMENT

bakers' trays, various

box grater

chinois (fine strainer for stocks)

digital scales with 1 gram/ounce increments up to 5 kilograms (11 lb)

funnels

glass mixing bowls

heavy duty baking sheets (e.g. solid teknics)

kitchen scissors

large kitchen spoons for shaping meringues, quenelles

measuring jugs

metal mixing bowls (e.g. 4 small, 4 medium, 4 large)

non-stick frying pans (Woll Diamond Lite are my go-to)

pastry brushes, various sizes

piping (pastry) bags

piping nozzles (pastry tips)

plastic scraper, metal scraper

rolling pin

rubber spatula

set of cup measures

set of spoon measures

sieves: regular, flour and drum

Silpat mats

tea strainers

whisks, various

wire racks with fitting trays

COOKING GEAR

baking dishes, heavy-based ceramic and steel

cast-iron pot, or Dutch oven (e.g. Le Creuset or Staub)

cast-iron frying pan

griddle plate

mandoline (e.g. Japanese Benriner)

non-stick frying pan

roasting trays

steel saucepans with lids, various sizes

APPLIANCES

food processor

hand-held blender

Japanese rice cooker

stand mixer

sandwich press

separate freezer in the garage!

spice grinder

MISCELLANEOUS

aluminium foil

baking paper

butcher's twine

cloth wipes (e.g. Chux)

plastic wrap

go-between freezer film

paper towel

marker pen

masking tape

piping bags, disposable

protective gloves, disposable

1 THE NEIGHBOURS

CANAPES / SNACKS SERVED ON ARRIVAL	Prawn cocktail lettuce cups
STARTERS SHARED AND SERVED AT THE SAME TIME	Kingfish, radishes, ginger and finger lime Smoked ocean trout, dill yoghurt, crunchy red onion
MAINS & SIDES SERVED TOGETHER ON THE TABLE	Sticky spicy short ribs Ginger corn rice Pickled cucumber and mint salad
DESSERT	Strawberry, rhubarb, mascarpone cream, salty chocolate, coconut meringue
WINE TIME	Blanc de Blancs Champagne Bone-dry riesling Dry chardonnay, Chablis style Bordeaux-style red blend (*decanted before serving*) 'Little Fizzer' Bugey de Cerdon (*best served chilled in white wine glasses*)
COCKTAIL HOUR	Martinez 210

I tested the recipes in this book every weekend for three months in my unrenovated home kitchen. It was important to me to use domestic appliances and equipment, to keep it approachable and achievable.

With some recipes being tested multiple times, we were producing a lot of food and were without a restaurant in which to serve it. We held dinner parties, of course, but the most rigorous testing took place during the day.

Thankfully my neighbours stepped up to the plate – quite literally, in many cases. I could not have done it without their help and support. They didn't think of themselves as guinea pigs, but rather, as willing collaborators, able to pitch in and help out their chef neighbour with open hearts and open mouths.

Not only did they help make the food disappear, they gave me their considered opinions as well. It felt like being back in the restaurant game again, having a street full of food critics, critiquing every dish (oh no, what have I done???). Feedback is everything to a chef, even more so when you are cooking food to be recreated at home, so I am very grateful.

My neighbours also helped my creative process, in that I tried to create this dinner party menu with them in mind, coming up with dishes that they might be familiar with, but not too familiar; inspiring, but not too left of centre. So there are prawn cocktail lettuce cups, and a main course of sticky, spicy short ribs that's crying out for that great bottle of red your guests brought. The aim is comfort food, elevated to the next level – especially when it comes to the dessert of strawberries, mascarpone cream, salty chocolate and coconut meringue, piled high and decadent.

Of course, it's always a good idea to keep the neighbours sweet (you never know when you may need them to feed your cat or water the garden). What if everyone who read this book invited their neighbours to dinner? That would be downright neighbourly.

THE PLAYLIST AIMEE MANN 'Magnolia': Music from the Motion Picture **THE ARCHITEC** Come from Heaven **THE CINEMATIC ORCHESTRA** Ma Fleur **LONDON GRAMMA SILVER ALERT** Etoile Polaire **PORTISHEAD** Dummy **ST GERMAIN** Tourist (Remastered

…oundations **ART OF NOISE** Reconstructed … For Your Listening Pleasure **ALPHA**
… You Wait **MAZZY STAR** So Tonight That I Might See **PHILIP GLASS AND**
…EAN-MICHEL JARRE Oxygène **TROUBLEMAKERS** Doubts & Convictions

Prawn cocktail lettuce cups

FROM THE PANTRY
Taberu rayu table chilli
(Basics, page 226)

DAY BEFORE

Make chilli lime mayonnaise
and refrigerate.

Pick out the best leaves
and refrigerate.

Peel prawns and refrigerate.

ON THE DAY

Cook prawns and cool.

Toss in chilli lime mayonnaise
and refrigerate.

Who doesn't love a prawn (shrimp) cocktail? This is a play on the classic, served in baby gem lettuce cups.

Your prawn options include buying whole prawns and cooking them yourself (save the shells in the freezer for your next shellfish oil), or purchasing green prawn meat. If you prefer to buy cooked prawns, make sure they are well drained, as any excess water will loosen the mayonnaise.

CHILLI LIME MAYONNAISE

100 g (3½ oz) Kewpie (QP) or whole egg mayonnaise
2 tablespoons Taberu rayu table chilli (Basics, page 226)
2 teaspoons Japanese tonkatsu sauce or HP sauce
2 tablespoons tomato ketchup
zest of 1 lime
2 teaspoons lime juice

Mix the mayonnaise with the taberu rayu, using the paste only, not the oil. — Add the tonkatsu or HP sauce, tomato ketchup, lime zest and lime juice, mixing well until combined. — Store in an airtight container in the refrigerator.

LETTUCE CUPS

4 baby gem lettuces
20 whole paradise or banana prawns (shrimp) (about 650 g/1 lb 7 oz), or 300 g (10½ oz) green prawn meat
1 tablespoon butter
125 g (4½ oz) Chilli lime mayonnaise, as above
1 teaspoon smoked sweet paprika

Trim the base of the baby gem lettuces and remove the large outer leaves. — Choose 14 of the best-shaped leaves, and reserve the remaining leaves for a salad. — Wash and drain the leaves, then store in an airtight container lined with paper towel and refrigerate. — If using whole prawns, peel the prawns and arrange them between layers of paper towel in an airtight container. Refrigerate for at least 6 hours before use. — Heat the butter in a frying pan until it begins to froth, and sauté the prawns or prawn meat gently until just cooked. — Set aside to cool, then refrigerate in an airtight container until chilled. — Once cold, cut the prawns into 1 cm (½ in) pieces, toss in chilli lime mayonnaise, and refrigerate. — To serve, arrange the lettuce cups on a tray, and fill each with one tablespoonful of the prawn mixture, mounded to give some height. — Lightly dust with paprika through a small, fine sieve and serve immediately.

Kingfish, radishes, ginger and finger lime

FROM THE PANTRY
Lime and rice-wine vinegar
(Basics, page 219)

DAY BEFORE
Prep finger limes.
Clean kingfish.

ON THE DAY
AM
Make lime and ginger dressing.
Dice radishes and hold in
iced water.

PM
Dice kingfish and refrigerate.

Although the kingfish is raw for this recipe, it's almost a kind of ceviche, in that it is lightly pickled by the fresh ginger and lime, keeping it fresh and zesty. Radish adds crunch and spice, making this a textural pleasure.

FINGER LIME PEARLS

3 finger limes, red or green	Cut the finger limes lengthways down the centre and use your thumb or a teaspoon to push out the pearls. — Discard any seeds, then store in an airtight container in the refrigerator.

LIME AND GINGER DRESSING

1 tablespoon grated ginger	Whisk the ginger into the lime vinegar. — Whisk in the olive oil and store in an airtight container in the refrigerator.
60 ml (2 fl oz) Lime and rice-wine vinegar (Basics, page 219)	
60 ml (2 fl oz) olive oil	

KINGFISH AND RADISHES

500 g (1 lb 2 oz) Spencer Gulf Hiramasa kingfish, loin and belly, skin removed	Trim the kingfish, making sure it's clean of any bloodline. — Cut the kingfish into 1 cm (½ in) dice, then refrigerate on a tray lined with paper towel. — Cut the radishes into ½ cm (¼ in) dice, and store in a container of iced water. — When ready to serve, drain the radish and dry on paper towel. — Mix with the lime and rice-wine vinegar and white sesame oil, stirring to coat. — Season with sea salt and set aside. — In a separate bowl, gently coat the diced kingfish with olive oil. — Season with white pepper, white soy sauce and half the finger lime pearls and fold through gently. (If you mix too hard, the fats in the fish will be released and become pasty.) — Divide the kingfish between cocktail glasses or serving bowls, pressing down gently. — Shake or whisk the lime and ginger dressing vigorously, and pour a spoonful over each serve, so that it pools evenly around the fish. — Add the remaining finger lime pearls to the radish mixture, then scatter evenly over the kingfish. — Serve immediately.
300 g (10½ oz) cherry belle radishes	
1 tablespoon Lime and rice-wine vinegar (Basics, page 219)	
2 teaspoons white sesame oil or avocado oil	
sea salt, to taste	
1 tablespoon extra-virgin olive oil (e.g. Alto Vividus)	
pinch ground white pepper	
2 teaspoons white soy sauce	
Finger lime pearls, as above	
Lime and ginger dressing, as above	

CHEF'S TIP
Prepare the various elements
ahead of time, and dress the
fish just before you serve, for
ultimate freshness.

Smoked ocean trout, dill yoghurt, crunchy red onion

PREP AHEAD
Hang yoghurt a few days prior.

DAY BEFORE
Make dill yoghurt.

ON THE DAY
AM
Grill baguette.

Slice onions
and refrigerate.

PM
Plate dill yoghurt and trout
30 minutes prior to guest arrival.

It's fun to have an interactive dish that you can invite your guests to build themselves. Here, they can pile smoked ocean trout onto crisp mini toasts with dill yoghurt and crunchy red onion. This is a great sharing dish that really helps break the ice.

DILL YOGHURT

500 g (1 lb 2 oz) goat's milk yoghurt
1 lemon, zested
2 tablespoons dill, lightly chopped
freshly milled black pepper

MAKES 350 g (12½ oz)

Line a sieve with a dampened sheet of muslin (cheesecloth) and set above a bowl. — Add the yoghurt to the sieve and refrigerate for around 5 hours. Around 150 g (5½ oz) of liquid whey will seep through the strainer. This can be reserved and used for dressings and vinaigrettes. — Pass the now-firm yoghurt through a fine sieve, then lightly whisk in the lemon zest, chopped dill and black pepper until well combined. Refrigerate in an airtight container.

MINI TOASTS

1 day-old baguette
100 ml (3½ fl oz) extra-virgin olive oil
sea salt and freshly milled black pepper

Heat a cast-iron griddle pan with ridges or barbecue until smoking hot. — Using a serrated knife, cut 12–14 thin slices of baguette, around 4–5 mm (¼ in) thick on a slight angle, making them around 6–7 cm (2½-2¾ in) long. — Brush both sides of each slice with olive oil and season with salt and pepper. — Grill until charred and toasted on both sides, then transfer to a wire rack until required.

TO SERVE

1 medium red onion, peeled
1 tablespoon chardonnay vinegar
1 tablespoon extra-virgin olive oil, plus extra to serve
sea salt and black pepper
150 g (5½ oz) Dill yoghurt, as above
cracked black pepper, to serve
400 g (14 oz) smoked ocean trout or salmon, sliced
1 lemon, for zesting
mini toasts, as above

Slice the red onion into 3 mm (⅛ in) thick rounds and separate the medium and small rings. — Lightly dress the onion rings with chardonnay vinegar and olive oil, season with a little salt and pepper, mix gently and set aside. — Spread the dill yoghurt onto the base of your serving platter. — Drizzle with a little extra olive oil and season with cracked black pepper. — Arrange slices of ocean trout over the yoghurt to cover, overlapping slightly. — Arrange the red onion randomly over the ocean trout and finish with a little extra olive oil, black pepper and lemon zest. — Serve with the mini toasts, inviting guests to place ocean trout, yoghurt and red onion on each toast.

CHEF'S TIP
Purchase mini toasts from a good delicatessen if you prefer.

Sticky spicy short ribs

FROM THE PANTRY

Fragrant chilli oil
(Basics, page 216)

Saucy romesco
(Basics, page 224)

PREP AHEAD

Make spice mix.

Braise short ribs up to
4 or 5 days ahead.

DAY BEFORE

Make glaze for ribs,
and refrigerate.

ON THE DAY

PM

Glaze ribs after the entrée,
allowing 45 minutes to complete.

This is the perfect dinner party main course! All the hard work is done, and can even be done days ahead. Seek out short ribs with a 3+ marble score, which you can purchase a week before you need them. Serve with Saucy romesco (page 224) for something refreshing and cooling on the side.

SHORT RIB SPICE MIX

½ teaspoon Indian coriander seeds
½ teaspoon coriander seeds
½ teaspoon yellow mustard seeds
½ teaspoon black peppercorns
½ teaspoon fennel seeds
½ teaspoon Sichuan peppercorns
½ teaspoon chilli flakes
1 teaspoon smoked sweet paprika

Toast the spices in a dry, small, heavy-based frying pan until fragrant. — Remove and put in a mortar. — Lightly crush all the spices together with a pestle, then set aside.

SHORT RIBS

1 × 3-bone short rib (weight with bone, 1.8 kg/4 lb)
1 teaspoon ground white pepper
30 ml (1 fl oz) vegetable oil
4 red onions, peeled and roughly chopped
3 teaspoons Short rib spice mix, as above, plus extra for the glaze
1 bird's eye chilli, split
30 g (1 oz) ginger, thinly sliced
4 garlic cloves, crushed
3 carrots, peeled and cut lengthways into quarters
80 g (2¾ oz) dark brown sugar
200 g (7 oz) honey
2 litres (68 fl oz) chicken stock
1 litre (34 fl oz) water
80 ml (2½ fl oz) soy sauce
120 g (4½ oz) tonkatsu, Bull-Dog or HP barbecue sauce

Heat the oven to 160°C (320°F). — Dust the short rib in the white pepper. — Heat a large, deep flameproof casserole dish (around 8 litres/270 fl oz), then add the vegetable oil and heat until hot. — Sear the short rib in the hot oil until caramelised on all sides. — Remove the rib and set aside. — Add the red onions to the dish and sauté over a medium heat until caramelised. — Add the spice mix, tossing well, and cook for 1 minute. — Add the chilli, ginger, garlic and carrots, tossing well. — Add the brown sugar and honey and cook until the mix starts to caramelise. — Add the chicken stock, water, soy sauce and tonkatsu sauce and bring to a simmer. — Simmer for 5–10 minutes, skimming the surface of any impurities.— Return the roasted short rib to the pan and make sure it is covered by liquid, topping up with water if needed. — Cover the pot with a lid and braise in the oven for around 2 hours, when the meat should still be firm to the touch. Remove some of the stock if needed so that the meat is just showing at the surface, then return the pot to the oven, uncovered, for a further hour. — Test for tenderness. If not tender, braise for a further 30 minutes (times will differ between different breeds and animal age). — When tender, gently pull out the bones and discard. — Leave the beef to rest in its braising liquid for 2–3 hours. — Remove the meat from the liquid, drain, and cut out any pockets of sinew and discard. — Strain the braising liquid into a clean saucepan. Add the meat and leave at room temperature until required, if cooking the same day. If cooking in advance, store in the refrigerator, up to 4 or 5 days ahead.

CHEF'S TIP

If you are cooking this 3 or 4 days ahead, make sure that once cooled, the rib is submerged in the cooking liquid and is kept in the coldest part of the refrigerator (down the bottom, at the back).

Heat the ribs 2 hours prior to guests arriving: warm some master stock, add the ribs and bake at 130°C (265°F) for 1-2 hours, then remove, drain and proceed to glaze, as above.

SHORT RIB GLAZE

65 g (2¼ oz) honey
remaining Short rib spice mix, as above
25 ml (¾ fl oz) black vinegar, or balsamic vinegar
30 ml (1 fl oz) orange juice
450 ml (15 fl oz) braising liquid master stock, as above
50 ml (1¾ fl oz) Fragrant chilli oil (Basics, page 216)
Saucy romesco, to serve (Basics, page 224)

Heat the honey in a small saucepan with the spice mix, stirring until the mixture caramelises. — Mix the black vinegar and orange juice and add to the honey mixture to stop it caramelising. — Bring to a simmer, add 250 ml (8½ fl oz) of the braising liquid and reduce to a thick glaze over a low heat. — Heat the oven to 185°C (365°F). Put the short ribs snugly into a small roasting tray, meat-side facing up. — Add the remaining 200 ml (7 fl oz) braising liquid and brush the meat with a little of the glaze. — Wrap with foil and hold until ready to serve. — Around 40 minutes before serving, heat the ribs in the oven for 15 minutes. — Discard the foil, and brush with the glaze every 5 minutes for a further 15 minutes, until the ribs are dark and caramelised. — Drizzle with the fragrant chilli oil and continue to baste with oil and glaze for a further 5 minutes. — Remove and rest for 5 minutes before serving. — Serve on a platter in the centre of the table.

Ginger corn rice

Buy a rice cooker! You'll never regret it.

DAY BEFORE
Remove corn from cob, and refrigerate with butter and ginger.

ON THE DAY
Wash rice and soak in the rice cooker for 30 minutes prior to cooking.

CHEF'S TIP
If you don't have a rice cooker, may I suggest you get one. It will make your life so much easier. Just prep the corn and ginger beforehand, mix with the soaked rice, and turn the rice on to cook when your guests arrive.

Rice is the perfect foil for big-flavour braised dishes like the short ribs, especially when it's fragrant with ginger and sweet with buttery corn. This dish uses my favourite go-to rice, Japanese koshihikari, a premium short-grain rice that keeps its shape beautifully.

CORN AND GINGER

1 fresh corn on the cob	
30 g (1 oz) grated fresh ginger	
50 g (1¾ oz) unsalted butter, chopped	

Clean the corn from its husk and cut the cob in half to make it easy to handle. — Stand each half cob on a board, cut-side down, and run the blade of a sharp knife down the corn to remove the kernels. Don't get too close to the core of the cob, as this will be too fibrous. — Set the kernels aside. — Over a bowl or tray, use the back of the knife to scrape down the core of the corn to remove all the starchy juices. — Combine the juices and kernels – you should have a total weight of around 150 g (5½ oz). — Add the ginger and butter to the corn, then store in an airtight container in the refrigerator until required.

TO COOK RICE

300 g (10½ oz) Japanese koshihikari rice	
300 ml (10 fl oz) filtered water	
Corn and ginger, as above	

Put the rice in a large bowl, then run cold water into the bowl until it is three-quarters full. — Using your hand, agitate the water with the rice until the water is cloudy with starch. — Drain off the water, and refill with clean, cold water. Repeat this process six times, or until the water runs clear. — In a rice cooker, combine the rice, filtered water, corn, ginger and butter and a good pinch of salt, stirring, then leave to soak for 30 minutes. — Set the cooker to sushi rice setting, and cook for around 1 hour. — Leave the rice on the 'keep warm' setting until required. — Lightly fluff the rice with a plastic spoon or spatula, then serve.

Pickled cucumber and mint salad

FROM THE PANTRY
Seasoned rice-wine vinegar (Basics, page 224)

DAY BEFORE
Pick mint leaves and store.

CHEF'S TIP
Cucumbers are over 90 per cent water. Stacking the slices back together will keep them moist and stop the juices coming out when stored.

A refreshing pickle that's easy to make and easy to eat. This is little more than freshly sliced cucumber that is ever so lightly pickled to order, and tossed with mint. It's also beautiful with fish dishes, grilled meats and Asian curries.

3 Lebanese (short) cucumbers	
25 ml (¾ fl oz) Seasoned rice-wine vinegar (Basics, page 224) or chardonnay vinegar	
sea salt	
30 g (1 oz/about 1 bunch) picked mint leaves	

Slice the cucumbers lengthways on a mandoline or with a vegetable peeler, giving you long strips around 2 mm (⅛ in) thick. — Line an airtight container with paper towel and stack the sliced cucumber together. Cover and refrigerate until required. — To serve, lay cucumber slices loosely in a bowl and season with vinegar and a little sea salt, mixing gently with your hand. — Lightly chop the mint and fold it through the cucumber, then arrange cucumber strips in a sculptural pattern on a serving platter.

Strawberry, rhubarb, mascarpone cream, salty chocolate, coconut meringue

PREP AHEAD

Make rhubarb compote up to 4 days ahead.

Stock up on coconut meringue biscuits.

Macerate strawberries up to 2–3 days ahead.

DAY BEFORE

Make mascarpone cream and chocolate chantilly.

ON THE DAY

Assemble a few hours in advance, add meringue biscuits when ready to serve.

I think this is one of those desserts that everyone will be talking about for weeks! It's based on an old English fool (not me, actually), or Eton Mess, and is served in elegant glassware. Piping bags make it even easier to achieve height and elegance, so give it a go.

You can have most of the elements prepped beforehand and just pull it together at the time, or even make it in the late afternoon. Change the fruit and berries depending on the season – peaches and raspberries are beautiful together – giving you a totally new dessert.

RHUBARB COMPOTE

8 thin rhubarb stalks, around 500 g (1 lb 2 oz)	
100 g (3½ oz) sugar	

Trim and wash the rhubarb, then pat dry. — Cut into 1–2 cm (½–¾ in) long pieces and sprinkle with the sugar. — Leave at room temperature for around 1 hour. — Pour the juices into a wide-bottomed saucepan and bring to a simmer over a medium–high heat. — Reduce the heat to low–medium then add the rhubarb to the pan. Simmer over gentle heat and cook slowly, stirring from time to time, until the rhubarb is soft – about 12–15 minutes. Add more sugar if the rhubarb is too tart.

MACERATED STRAWBERRIES

750 g (1 lb 11 oz) fresh strawberries	
50 g (1¾ oz) caster (superfine) sugar	
1 teaspoon vanilla paste	

Rinse the strawberries, remove the stems and pat dry on paper towel. — Cut into quarters, then toss with the sugar and vanilla until evenly coated. — Leave to stand for at least 30 minutes, then refrigerate in an airtight container for 24–48 hours. — When the strawberries have released a lot of their juices, strain the juice into a small saucepan and simmer until reduced to a syrup. — Pour this syrup back over the strawberries and refrigerate until required.

MASCARPONE CREAM

300 g (10½ oz) thickened (whipping) cream	
35 g (1¼ oz) icing (confectioners') sugar, sifted	
½ teaspoon vanilla paste	
pinch of sea salt	
250 g (9 oz) mascarpone cheese	

Pour 250 g (9 oz) of the cream into a stand mixer and add the sifted icing sugar, vanilla paste and salt. — Whip to soft peaks. — In a separate bowl, mix the remaining 50 g (1¾ oz) cream with the mascarpone to soften. — Add the mascarpone mixture to the soft whipped cream and continue to whip until the mixture forms firm, stiff peaks. Be careful not to over-whip. — Scrape the cream into a piping bag, tie off the end, and refrigerate until required.

CHEF'S TIP

Valrhona Dulcey is a blonde, caramelised chocolate with a hauntingly beautiful flavour that I prefer to use in the place of white chocolate. Try it, you'll be hooked.

SALTED DULCEY BLOND CHOCOLATE CHANTILLY

1 leaf gelatine, gold strength

745 g (1 lb 10 oz) thickened (whipping) cream

1 teaspoon vanilla paste

1 level teaspoon sea salt

260 g (9 oz) Valrhona 32% Dulcey Blond chocolate, chopped

Soak the gelatine leaf in cold water for 3 minutes. — Meanwhile, boil 230 g (8 oz) of the cream with the vanilla and salt, stirring. Once boiled, remove from the heat. — Squeeze excess water from the gelatine, add to the boiled cream and stir until dissolved. — Put the chocolate in a heatproof bowl and pour the boiled cream on top. — Bring it together with a spatula until smooth (if not fully melted, put the bowl over a saucepan of hot water). — Once smooth, add the remaining 515 g (1 lb 2 oz) of cold cream and blend with a hand-held blender. — Refrigerate for 6 hours to set slightly. — When ready, pour the cold chocolate cream into the bowl of a stand mixer fitted with a whisk attachment, and whip to medium–firm peaks. — Transfer to a piping bag, tie off the end, and refrigerate until required.

TO SERVE

Rhubarb compote (page 34)

Mascarpone cream (page 34)

Macerated strawberries (page 34)

Salted Dulcey Blond chocolate chantilly, as above

12 coconut meringue biscuits, such as brutti e buoni

Spoon a little of the rhubarb compote into the base of six serving glasses. — Pipe the mascarpone cream on top, to cover. — Spoon a layer of macerated strawberries on top, adding plenty of strawberry syrup. — Pipe the chocolate chantilly on top, followed by a few more strawberries. — Crush the coconut meringue biscuits, scatter over the top, and serve.

EVERYONE WILL BE TALKING ABOUT THIS DESSERT

2 LOST IN TRANSLATION

**CANAPES /
SNACKS**
SERVED ON ARRIVAL

Spanner crab, yuzu kosho sandos
Salty chips, smoked roe, wasabi crème fraîche

STARTERS
SERVED AS
INDIVIDUAL DISHES

Tataki of kingfish, smoky 'nduja, piquillo peppers
Lobster, udon, shellfish oil

MAINS & SIDES
SERVED TOGETHER
ON THE TABLE

Chargrilled beef tenderloin, kabayaki sauce
Mushroom nori rice
Leaves, plum and apple balsamic

DESSERT

Meringues, yuzu curd, pistachio sherbet

WINE TIME

Non-vintage Champagne
Citrus and bitter Koshu (*Grace Wine is a sensational option*)
Junmai Daiginjo sake (*best served chilled*)
Barbera with liquorice and dry herb notes (*decanted before serving*)
German eiswein

COCKTAIL HOUR Whisky Sour 210

The modern cult movie classic *Lost in Translation* is one of my all-time favourite films. I've watched it multiple times since it premiered in 2003, and every time, I fall in love with the energy, enthusiasm and mystery of one of the most magical cities in the world: Tokyo. The movie forces you to feel the intimacy of human connection, of love, loss and disorientation, and to remember those sleepless nights in a new city, and a new culture. But I also find out more about myself; I find it leads me to question who am I, where am I, why am I here?

Sofia Coppola describes the storyline as 'things being disconnected, and looking for moments of connection' – something we can all relate to in one way or another.

For me, the movie sums up how I go through life; so much so that I use 'lost in translation' as a life statement. You either get me, or you don't. Either way is okay.

This menu was inspired by the parallels between Japanese and Australian food culture. It sets spanner crab sandos with a tangy yuzu kosho mayo, next to salty chips with smoked roe and wasabi crème fraîche. Char-grilled beef is hit with sansho pepper, and luxurious lobster is paired with the humble udon noodle.

The menu combines old and new, east and west, but underpinning it all is the Japanese philosophy of restraint, and of allowing things to be themselves. Start with the freshest quality produce and don't try to change its nature, but instead work with it, to elevate it.

This is food that's looking for moments of connection, coming together on your table, among friends, having fun. Perhaps I should have called it Found in Translation.

THE PLAYLIST SEX PISTOLS Never Mind the Bollocks **PRETENDERS** Pretenders **TH** The Teaches of Peaches **THE JESUS AND MARY CHAIN** Psychocandy **SÉBASTIE TV EYES** TV Eyes **SQUAREPUSHER** Ultravisitor

HEMICAL BROTHERS Come with Us **PATTI SMITH** Land (1975–2002) **PEACHES**
ELLIER L'incroyable Vérité **AIR** Talkie Walkie **DEATH IN VEGAS** Scorpio Rising

Spanner crab, yuzu kosho sandos

DAY BEFORE

Make yuzo kosho mayonnaise
and refrigerate.

ON THE DAY

AM

Cook crabmeat and cool,
fold through mayonnaise
and refrigerate.

Trim mustard cress and store.

PM

Make sandos, wrap in plastic
wrap and refrigerate.

30 MINUTES PRIOR

Cut into shapes and keep
at room temperature,
covered with a damp cloth.

These little clouds of soft white bread filled with lightly spiced crab mayonnaise will have the street talking. If you can't get raw crabmeat, use cooked fresh crabmeat instead; just be sure to drain it well or it will loosen the structure of the mayonnaise.

YUZU KOSHO MAYONNAISE

50 g (1¾ oz) Kewpie (QP) mayonnaise
30 g (1 oz) crème fraîche or sour cream
pinch of yuzu kosho or chilli paste, to taste
zest of ½ lemon

To make the yuzu kosho mayonnaise, combine the mayonnaise, crème fraîche, yuzu kosho and lemon zest and whisk well to combine. Refrigerate until required.

SPANNER CRAB

250 g (9 oz) raw spanner crabmeat
50 g (1¾ oz) butter

Place the crabmeat on a tray and check that there is no shell within the meat. — Heat the butter in a wide, heavy-based saucepan over a low–medium heat. — Once bubbling, add the crabmeat and toss it gently in the butter for a minute or two, being careful not to break up the delicate meat, until just cooked. — Drain the crab in a sieve set over a bowl, to remove the excess butter. — Set aside and cool at room temperature.

SANDOS

cooked crab, as above
Yuzu kosho mayonnaise, as above
6 slices milk bread, or soft white sliced bread
100 g (3½ oz) butter, softened
40 g (1½ oz) mustard cress

Fold the spanner crabmeat into the yuzu kosho mayonnaise and adjust the seasoning to taste. — Refrigerate until ready to use. — Lay the bread out on the bench top and spread each slice with butter. — Spread three slices with the crab mayonnaise. — Trim the mustard cress at the base of the punnet and scatter evenly over the crab. — Top with the remaining slices of bread, pressing gently. — Wrap each sandwich in plastic wrap and refrigerate until required. — Remove from the refrigerator 30 minutes before serving. — Remove the crusts from the sandos and cut into little triangles. — Keep covered with damp paper towel until ready to serve.

CHEF'S TIP

Feel free to cut into finger
sandwiches or stamp out
rounds instead of triangles.

Salty chips, smoked roe, wasabi crème fraîche

Prep salmon roe and
mix crème fraîche.

ON THE DAY
Dress salmon roe.

Plate dish 20 minutes
before guests arrive.

Smoked salmon roe is one of life's little luxuries, and I was one of its earliest adopters, smoking my own roe for restaurant guests at Sepia. Team its rich, subtly smoky oiliness with a velvety cream suffused with the heat of wasabi, and serve with salty potato crisps, and watch your guests go back for more. And more.

200 g (7 oz) smoked salmon roe, or cured salmon roe
zest of 1 lemon
1 tablespoon smoked olive oil, store bought
200 g (7 oz) crème fraîche or sour cream
2 teaspoons wasabi paste
100 g (3½ oz) sea salt potato chips (crisps)

Put the roe in a sieve and set over a bowl to drain. — Cover with plastic wrap and refrigerate for 2 hours. — Transfer the roe to a bowl and add the lemon zest and smoked olive oil. — Turn gently with a spoon until coated, then refrigerate in an airtight container until required. — Mix the crème fraîche and wasabi and taste (add more wasabi if you like it hot), then refrigerate in an airtight container until required. — Serve the wasabi crème fraîche, the smoked roe and the chips in separate bowls. Spoon some crème fraîche onto your chip, top with some roe and enjoy!

CHEF'S TIP
Smoked salmon roe is available from several excellent producers (or substitute with caviar for some really luxe chippies). You can use a plain roe, but if you do, consider marinating it in something interesting and non-acidic, such as beetroot juice or sake.

Tataki of kingfish, smoky 'nduja, piquillo peppers

FROM THE PANTRY

Sweet smoked paprika oil
(Basics, page 226)

PREP AHEAD

Pre-order kingfish
from fishmonger.

DAY BEFORE

Make 'nduja dressing.

Clean kingfish and store.

ON THE DAY

AM

Sear kingfish in sansho pepper,
wrap and refrigerate.

PM

Slice kingfish and refrigerate.

Kingfish is one of the most versatile and sustainable fish we have in Australia, coming from the largest producer of aquaculture kingfish outside of Japan. Having worked closely with Clean Seas' Spencer Gulf Hiramasa kingfish for many years, I prize it highly for its sashimi quality, and for its fresh, clean taste. The flesh is firm, pinky-white, holds its texture when sliced, and even holds up to this rich, oily, spicy, Spanish-inspired dressing. (If I sound like a fan, I am.)

You'll need 800 g (1 lb 12 oz) kingfish for this recipe – I suggest you order a 1.2 kg (2 lb 10 oz) fillet, and save the rich belly meat for another recipe. Or replace with salmon, tuna or albacore.

'NDUJA

100 g (3½ oz) 'nduja salami	
60 g (2 oz) drained and cleaned piquillo peppers (e.g. Navarrico)	
30 ml (1 fl oz) olive oil	
60 g (2 oz) shallots, finely chopped	
1 garlic clove, finely chopped	
30 ml (1 fl oz) sherry vinegar	
60 ml (2 fl oz) Sweet smoked paprika oil (Basics, page 226)	

Break the 'nduja up into small pieces, and cut the piquillo peppers into small dice, around 5 mm (¼ in). — Set the 'nduja and the peppers aside in separate bowls. — Heat the olive oil in a heavy-based saucepan over a medium heat. — Add the shallots and garlic, and sauté until lightly coloured and transparent. — Add the 'nduja and sauté until the oils separate from the meat. — Add the sherry vinegar and smoked paprika oil and season well. — Remove from the heat, add the peppers, then set aside.

KINGFISH

800 g (1 lb 12 oz) loin Spencer Gulf Hiramasa kingfish	
1 tablespoon sansho pepper, or white pepper	
30 ml (1 fl oz) olive oil	
sea salt	

To prep the kingfish, cut the loin in half, and trim off any bloodline, scales, pin bones and sinew. — Wrap each piece in paper towel, then wrap in plastic wrap and refrigerate for at least 6 hours to draw out excess moisture. — Unwrap and dust liberally with sansho pepper until coated all over. — Heat a large non-stick frying pan over a low–medium heat, then add the olive oil. — Lightly sear the kingfish on all sides so that the outside flesh turns white and becomes firm to the touch. The pan shouldn't be too hot, as you don't want a hard crust on the fish. — Drain on paper towel and allow to cool, then wrap in fresh paper towel and refrigerate until required.

TO SERVE

Unwrap the kingfish and slice into 5 mm (¼ in) thick slices, on a slight angle. — Arrange the slices in a circular pattern on a high-edged plate, starting on the outside and working all the way around the plate. — Gently warm the 'nduja and piquillo peppers over a low heat. Add a little more sherry and paprika oil if the mixture looks dry. — Spoon the 'nduja dressing into the centre of the plate and serve immediately.

CHEF'S TIP

Sansho pepper is a fragrant, citrussy, spicy Japanese pepper with a little tingle.

THE DINNER PARTY

Lobster, udon, shellfish oil

FROM THE PANTRY

Shellfish oil (Basics, page 225)

DAY BEFORE

Blanch and clean lobster.

ON THE DAY

Prep ingredients an
hour in advance.

Lobster takes udon noodles to the next level in this wonderfully indulgent recipe, fit for a special occasion or celebration. But the real hero here is the shellfish oil, which adds so much flavour. Make it ahead and keep in the refrigerator for up to two months, or freeze for up to 12 months, and use in dressings, or add to mayonnaise for a special cocktail sauce. You can swap the lobster for prawns (shrimp), or change the udon noodles to angel hair pasta or linguine if you prefer.

PREPARING THE LOBSTER

1 kg (2 lb 3 oz) live lobster

To stun the lobster, put it in the freezer for about 30 minutes. — Once the lobster is sleepy, place it on a chopping board and pierce the tip of a sharp knife between the eyes and the centre of the head to kill it quickly. — Cut between the body and the head and twist off the tail, making sure to cut right into the head cavity to collect all the meat. — Bring a pot of salted water to the boil and blanch the lobster tail for 30 seconds. — Remove the lobster and refresh in iced water. — Once cool, use scissors to cut along each side of the belly before the top shell starts, where it is softer, and pull the belly shell part away. — Use your thumb to push under the top shell, between meat and shell, and remove the tail meat. — Remove the intestinal tract from the tail meat, then place the tail meat on paper towel to dry off excess moisture. — You should have around 330 g (11½ oz) of lobster meat. Wrap in fresh paper towel, then tightly in plastic wrap, and refrigerate until required.

FLAVOURED SHELLFISH OIL

150 ml (5 fl oz) Shellfish oil
(Basics, page 225)

3 tablespoons chopped
tarragon leaves

25 g (1 oz) finely chopped chives

1 tablespoon shio kombu (salted
kombu, e.g. Fujicco shio)

½ teaspoon salt

¼ teaspoon sugar

¼ teaspoon white pepper

½ teaspoon sansho pepper

1 teaspoon mirin

1 teaspoon white soy sauce

300–330 g (10½–11½ oz) lobster
meat, as above

In a large bowl, combine all the ingredients except the lobster, mixing well. — Cut the lobster meat in half lengthways, and cut into thin slices. — Fold the lobster into the shellfish oil until well coated, and refrigerate, covered, until required.

TO SERVE

240 g (8½ oz) dried udon noodles

prepared lobster in shellfish oil,
as above

1 tablespoon butter

Bring a large (e.g. 6 litre/202 fl oz) pot of salted water to a rolling boil. — Cook the noodles for 4 minutes or until tender but still chewy. — Gently cook the lobster and shellfish oil in a wide-based saucepan over a medium heat until fragrant, without frying too hard. — Add the butter and stir through. — Drain the noodles and rinse under hot running water to wash off the starch. — Shake well to drain off excess water. — Add the noodles to the pan, tossing well to coat – add more shellfish oil if the mixture feels dry. — Use tongs to divide the noodles and lobster between warm bowls and serve immediately.

CHEF'S TIP

When preparing the lobster,
save all the shells and freeze,
so you can make shellfish
oil in the future.

Chargrilled beef tenderloin, kabayaki sauce

FROM THE PANTRY

Kabayaki sauce
(Basics, page 217)

Rendered beef fat
(Basics, page 222) or Clarified
butter (Basics, page 215)

Pickled red onions for
everything (Basics, page 221)

Benno's hot miso mustard
(Basics, page 214)

DAY BEFORE

Remove beef from packaging,
wrap in paper towel and
refrigerate overnight.

ON THE DAY

Uncover beef and refrigerate.

Take beef to room temperature
for 2 hours prior to cooking.

CHEF'S TIP

Once the meat has reached the
core temperature of 54°C (130°F),
leave it to cool in the fat in a
warm place. If you prefer it be
cooked further to medium-rare,
leave until it reaches 60°C (140°F),
or to 68°C (155°F) for medium–
well. (A meat thermometer is your
best friend when cooking larger
pieces of meat.)

To re-use the fat or clarified
butter, strain into a container
and refrigerate. Once set,
remove, drain off any liquid
and pat dry with paper towel.
Melt over a medium heat until
all moisture is removed, then
cool and store in the freezer
for next time.

Kabayaki is a sweet soy glaze, traditionally used for unagi (eel) in Japan, but it adds a wonderful sweet and savoury note to a beautiful piece of beef. Feel free to use tenderloin from grass-fed or grain-fed animals, from Angus to Wagyu, of whatever marble score you like. This method of low and slow cooking in beef fat or butter lets you relax as much as the beef does, and searing it first on a barbecue adds a lovely smokiness.

PREPARING THE BEEF

1–1.2 kg (2 lb 3 oz–2 lb 10 oz)
beef tenderloin, centre cut
(trimmed weight)

The day before, remove the beef from any packaging, wipe with paper towel, roll in fresh paper towel and refrigerate overnight. — The next day, remove the beef and cut lengthways to give you two long strips, flatter rather than rounder. — Place the beef on a rack, uncovered, and return to the refrigerator. — One to two hours prior to cooking, remove and leave at room temperature.

COOKING THE BEEF

1 kg (2 lb 3 oz) Rendered beef fat
(Basics, page 222) or Clarified
butter (Basics, page 215), melted

1 tablespoon sansho pepper
or ground white pepper

Heat the oven to 80°C (175°F). — Put the rendered beef fat or clarified butter in a roasting tray that will hold the beef snugly, and heat in the oven for 20 minutes, until melted. — Brush the beef with the melted beef fat or clarified butter and dust with the sansho pepper. — Heat the barbecue to high, and sear the fillets well on all sides until caramelised. — Transfer the beef to the roasting tray and submerge it carefully in the fat, then put in the oven. — Bake for around 1 hour, or until the internal core temperature of the meat reaches 54°C (130°F). — Remove, cover with aluminium foil, and leave in a warm place for up to 1 hour, or keep warm in the oven at 50°C (120°F).

TO SERVE

100 g (3½ oz) Kabayaki sauce
(Basics, page 217)

Pickled red onions for everything
(Basics, page 221)

Benno's hot miso mustard
(Basics, page 214)

When ready to serve, remove the beef and drain on a rack set over a tray. — Warm the kabayaki sauce in a small saucepan and brush over the beef until well coated. You may like to warm the beef through in the oven for 10 minutes before serving. — Carve into even slices 1 cm (½ in) thick and arrange on a warm serving dish. — Brush with more kabayaki sauce and serve immediately with pickled red onions for everything and Benno's hot miso mustard on the side.

Mushroom nori rice

DAY BEFORE
Prep the mushrooms,
then refrigerate in an
airtight container.

ON THE DAY
Slice the nori, soak the rice
in stock and mushrooms
before cooking.

CHEF'S TIP
If you want light and fluffy
grains for braised rice, coconut
rice or sushi rice, rinse the rice
well before cooking, but if you
want creamy rice for risotto or
rice pudding, don't wash it at all.

Many people are a little scared of cooking rice, and I can understand why. It can be one of the simplest and one of the most difficult things to cook.

But really, it's all about understanding the type of rice that you are using, and the dish you are cooking. A rice cooker will take all the pain out of cooking rice – and keep it warm for you as well.

PREPARING THE MUSHROOMS

320 g (11½ oz) mixed mushrooms (oysters, shimeji, king brown)
100 g (3½ oz) butter, unsalted

Tear the mushrooms into pieces or cut them into quarters, depending on the type. — Heat half the butter in a large frying pan and sauté half the mushrooms over a high heat until they start to caramelise and soften. — Tip the butter and mushrooms into a bowl. — Repeat with the remaining butter and mushrooms.

COOKING THE RICE

380 g (13½ oz) koshihikari sushi rice
buttery mushrooms, as above
450 ml (15 fl oz) Mushroom stock (Basics, page 220)
1 teaspoon truffle paste
2 sheets toasted nori, cut into fine strips

Put the rice in a large bowl and run cold running water into the bowl until three-quarters full. — Using your hand, agitate the water with the rice until the water is cloudy with starch. — Drain off the water, and refill with clean, cold water. — Repeat this process six times, or until the water runs clear, then put the rice in a rice cooker. — Add the cooked mushrooms and all their buttery juices, mushroom stock and truffle paste, stirring, and leave to soak for 30 minutes. — Set the cooker to the sushi rice setting and cook for around 1 hour. — Leave the rice on the 'keep warm' setting until required. — To serve, lightly fluff the rice with a plastic spoon or spatula and scatter with strips of nori.

Leaves, plum and apple balsamic

PREP AHEAD
Make apple balsamic and plum
vinegar up to a few weeks prior.

ON THE DAY
Make dressing and leave
at room temperature.

CHEF'S TIP
Salted plum paste or umeboshi
is a Japanese staple, available
from all good Asian food stores.
If you don't have it, use tamarind
paste or pomegranate molasses
instead.

Whenever I serve a steak or roast meat, I also serve a salad, usually one with a light, slightly acidic and sweet dressing, to help cut the richness of the meat. Peppery leaves such as mizuna, watercress and wild rocket are my favourites, but feel free to use the ones you love.

PLUM AND APPLE BALSAMIC VINEGAR

150 ml (5 fl oz) balsamic vinegar
150 ml (5 fl oz) clear apple juice
2 granny smith apples or other tart cooking apples
50 g (1¾ oz) umeboshi salted plum paste

Pour the balsamic vinegar and apple juice into a small saucepan. — Core the apples, then cut into slices and add to the balsamic and apple juice. — Bring the mixture to a boil, then simmer gently until the liquid is reduced to around 200 ml (7 fl oz). — Strain through a fine sieve, pressing down on the apples to extract as much flavour as possible. — Set the vinegar to one side and allow to cool. — Add the plum paste and blend until smooth, using a hand-held blender. — Refrigerate in an airtight container for up to 1 month.

DRESSING

60 ml (2 fl oz) Plum and apple balsamic vinegar, as above
60 ml (2 fl oz) olive oil
sea salt and pepper
150 g (5½ oz) mixed salad leaves

To make the dressing, put the plum and apple balsamic vinegar in a jar with the olive oil, salt and pepper and shake well to emulsify. — Put the mixed leaves in a large bowl, pour the dressing over and toss gently with your hands, or with tongs. — Serve immediately.

Meringues, yuzu curd, pistachio sherbet

What a pile of fun! These French-style meringues are one of Vicki's favourite desserts, with their crisp and crunchy exterior and soft marshmallow centres. Dusted with a bright green, tongue-tingling pistachio sherbet, these come with a built-in surprise: a creamy heart of tangy yuzu curd. Serve as a towering centrepiece on the table and invite everyone to help themselves. So good.

YUZU CURD

110 ml (4 fl oz) yuzu juice (or lemon or lime juice)
pinch of sea salt
110 g (4 oz) caster (superfine) sugar
120 g (4½ oz) egg yolks (from about 7 eggs)
250 g (9 oz) unsalted butter, chilled and diced

MAKES 480 G (1 LB 1 OZ)

Combine the yuzu juice and salt in a heavy-based saucepan and bring to the boil. — Whisk the sugar and egg yolks together until pale in colour. — Pour the yuzu juice over the egg yolks, whisking constantly to incorporate. — Return the mixture to the pan and gently heat over a low–medium heat, stirring continuously, until the mixture reaches 84°C (185°F). — Strain the mixture into a clean bowl. — Start adding the diced butter, whisking continuously, until all the butter is melted and the consistency is smooth. — Top the mixture with a sheet of baking paper to stop a skin from forming, then cover and refrigerate overnight until set. — The next day, whisk the mixture until smooth. Scrape into a piping (pastry) bag with a number 8 nozzle and tie off the end. Refrigerate until required.

PISTACHIO SHERBET

100 g (3½ oz) Iranian pistachios, whole or slivered
½ teaspoon citric acid
¼ teaspoon bicarbonate of soda (baking soda)
100 g (3½ oz) pure icing (confectioners') sugar

MAKES 200 G (7 OZ)

Pour half the pistachios into a spice grinder (they won't all fit at once), add the citric acid and bicarbonate of soda and blend to a fine powder. — Add half the icing sugar and blend again, until the mixture is a fine powder. — Pour into a bowl, then repeat with the remaining pistachios and sugar. — Mix the two powders together and strain through a sieve. — Any pistachio that won't pass through the sieve can be returned to the spice grinder with a teaspoon of the sieved powder. Blend this again on full speed until reduced to a fine powder, then add it to the original amount. — Store in an airtight container until required.

MERINGUES

220 g (8 oz) egg whites at room temperature (from about 6 eggs)
pinch of salt
¼ teaspoon cream of tartar
220 g (8 oz) caster (superfine) sugar
220 g (8 oz) icing (confectioners') sugar, sieved

Line two baking trays with Silpat mats or baking paper. — Heat the oven to 90°C (195°F). — Put the egg whites and salt into the bowl of a stand mixer and beat for about 10 seconds, until the whites break down. — Add the cream of tartar and beat until light and foamy. Continue to beat until the mixture reaches soft peaks. — Add the caster sugar slowly, in batches, continuing to whip until the whites are glossy and the mixture forms hard peaks. — Fold through the icing sugar in three batches, using a spatula, until smooth and glossy. — Using a large kitchen spoon, place 12 large scoops of the mixture onto the two trays. — Bake in the oven for around 3 hours. Remove onto a wire rack and allow to cool completely. — Once cooled, store in a large airtight container lined with paper towel. — The meringues will hold for 2–3 days in a cool dark place.

TO SERVE

Meringues, as above
Yuzu curd, as above
Pistachio sherbet, as above

Working one at a time, take a meringue and make a hole through the side using a skewer. — Remove the piping bag of yuzu curd from the refrigerator, gently push the nozzle into the hole in the meringue and fill the centre with the curd. — Repeat with the remaining meringues. — Lightly brush each meringue with a little of the remaining curd. — To serve, arrange the meringues in a tower on a serving platter, dusting with pistachio sherbet as you go. When the tower is complete, add a final dusting of pistachio sherbet. — Serve immediately.

A BUILT-IN SURPRISE

3 WHEN IN DOUBT, CHOOSE RED

CANAPES / SNACKS SERVED ON ARRIVAL	Tomato tartare on toast
STARTERS SERVED AS INDIVIDUAL DISHES	Tiger prawns, Campari rhubarb, finger lime Negroni rigatoni
MAINS & SIDES SERVED TOGETHER ON THE TABLE	Lamb shanks, pomegranate, charred cayenne peppers 'Better than hasselback' potatoes Radicchio, vincotto red onion
DESSERT	Raspberry, salted white chocolate
WINE TIME	Blanc de Noirs Champagne Medium-bodied pecorino (*best to carafe wine before serving*) Rose and leather Piedmont Nebbiolo Medium-bodied Cabernet Franc (*Loire Valley if possible*) Vibrant Moscato D'asti
COCKTAIL HOUR	Classic Negroni 210

It happened like this. We suddenly decided to throw a dinner party, and I had no idea what to cook. This is that precious moment I love, when all your senses are heightened, and you're open to what the universe may offer.

It was autumn, and the days were getting cooler, the nights drawing in. The leaves turned from scarlet to amber, then they curled and floated to the ground, and in the evening, the sky was ablaze, enriched by a fiery cloak of cardinal red.

It was this autumnal inspiration that I used to create a dessert of leaves for my restaurant Sepia in 2012, and the famous Toffee Apple for the *MasterChef* final in 2020. But there are now so many interpretations of those dishes out there, I wanted to go beyond them.

This is what creativity is for a chef: to be inspired by what is around us, and what nature is giving us, not only in terms of the produce, but also in life – the colours, the smells, the textures. It's how unforgettable pairings come about; like matching sweet prawns with a super-tangy dressing of rhubarb, Campari and finger limes; or turning the spicy warmth of a Negroni cocktail into a cheesy, creamy pasta sauce.

Red is such a celebratory autumn colour, shining through the fruits and vegetables of the season. Tomatoes are sweeter in autumn, peppers and capsicums are at their best, berries are abundant, and autumnal lettuces such as radicchio have the slight bitterness you need.

Run with it. Start with a glass of rosé Champagne, or a classic Negroni cocktail, and indulge your love of red wines against a rich background of lamb shanks and roasted potatoes. Consider theming the table with red cloth napkins, red water glasses and red chopsticks. Or don't theme it at all. Just let the vivid colours of the paprika-dusted potatoes – so much better than hasselback – and the raspberry tart stand out against an all-black or all-white table.

If your friends are up for anything, as ours are, then let them know the theme, and they might even dress accordingly. As Mr Bowie says, put on your red shoes, and dance the blues ... Just clear the tabletop first, maybe.

rfer Rosa ('Brick is Red') **PETER GABRIEL** So ('Red Rain') **ELVIS COSTELLO** My Aim
lk that Talk ('Red Lipstick') **KATE BUSH** The Red Shoes ('The Red Shoes') **RED HOT**
AVID BOWIE Let's Dance **GRACE JONES** Portfolio (La Vie En Rose)

Tomato tartare on toast

FROM THE PANTRY
Taberu rayu table chilli, if using
(Basics, page 226)

DAY BEFORE
Make semi-dried tomatoes.
Make tartare mix and refrigerate.

ON THE DAY
Make Turkish toasts and store.

As much as I love Japanese food, Spanish food also has a very special place in my heart. This dish happened by accident, when I wanted to do my version of the Spanish *pan con tomate* – basically grilled bread rubbed with tomato and its seeds, and doused in rich olive oil.

But I wanted to concentrate the flavour of the tomatoes, so I semi-dried them – and as so often happens, the end result was a complete surprise.

The semi-drying gives the tomatoes a slightly dry texture outside and a chewy texture inside, making them look, and even taste, like beef tartare. I swear if you closed your eyes, you couldn't tell the difference. Not what I was expecting, but so delicious, I had to share it.

TO PREPARE TOMATOES

1 kg (2 lb 3 oz) roma (plum) tomatoes, dark, red and ripe

MAKES 350 G (12½ OZ)

Fill a heavy-based 6 litre (203 fl oz) pot with water and bring to the boil. — Fill a large deep bowl with ice and water and set to one side. — Using a small, sharp knife, make an X on the bottom of each tomato, just enough to pierce the skin. — Using a spider or slotted spoon, lower the tomatoes, two or three at a time, into the boiling water. — Blanch for around 15–20 seconds, or until you see the skin start to peel around the X. Be careful not to blanch for too long, or the tomato will become mushy and grainy. — Plunge the tomatoes into the iced water and leave to completely cool. — Repeat with the remaining tomatoes. — Once all the tomatoes are blanched, remove from the iced water and drain onto a tray. — Using a small paring knife, peel away the skin. It should come off easily. — Pat dry with paper towel and place the skinned tomatoes on a chopping board. — Using a sharp knife, cut each tomato into quarters, slicing vertically from the stem to the base. — Carefully cut between the seeds and the flesh of the tomato, creating tomato petals. Reserve the seeds and set aside. — Place the petals on a tray lined with paper towel. Cover with another sheet of paper towel to absorb excess water, and refrigerate until required.

SEMI-DRIED TOMATOES

40 ml (1¼ fl oz) olive oil

1 shallot, peeled and finely diced

1 garlic clove, peeled and finely diced

freshly milled black pepper

Heat the oven to 105°C (220°F). — Heat the olive oil in a small heavy-based saucepan and, once hot, add the shallot and garlic. — Sauté over a low heat until the shallot is soft and transparent. — Season with black pepper and set to one side. — Line a tray and place a wire rack on top. — Arrange the tomato petals on the rack so that the side that had the skin on it faces down, forming a cup. — Add a spoonful of the shallot mix to each of the tomato petals. — Dry in the oven for around 2 hours until softened and dehydrated. — Remove and allow to cool, then dice and set aside.

TOMATO SEED SAUCE

good pinch of sea salt

tomato seeds, as above

Add sea salt to the tomato seeds, tossing well, and leave to sit for 20 minutes. This will leach out the juices. — Strain the juices through a fine sieve, pressing as much of the juice as possible through the sieve – you should end up with around 100 ml (3½ fl oz). — Pour the juice into a small saucepan and bring to the boil. Simmer until reduced to around 35 ml (1¼ fl oz), or one-third of its original volume, and set aside.

TURKISH TOASTS

2 pide (Turkish/flat bread)

100 ml (3½ fl oz) extra-virgin olive oil

sea salt

TOMATO TARTARE MIX

160 g (5½ oz) diced semi-dried tomatoes, as above

2 tablespoons Tomato seed sauce, page 65

2 teaspoons tonkatsu sauce

1 tablespoon tomato ketchup

2 teaspoons Dijon mustard

2 teaspoons Taberu rayu table chilli or chilli paste, optional (Basics, page 226)

Turkish toasts, as above

CHEF'S TIP:
This makes a great vegetarian course to serve as an alternative entrée.

Heat a sandwich press or barbecue. — Cut the bread into 1 cm (½ in) thick slices – you should have around 18 slices. — Brush with olive oil, put into the sandwich press and toast until golden. — Place on a tray lined with paper towel, season with salt and allow to cool completely. — Store in a sealed container until ready to serve.

MAKES 220 G (8 OZ)

In a bowl, whisk the diced semi-dried tomatoes with the tomato seed sauce, tonkatsu sauce, tomato ketchup, Dijon mustard and taberu rayu, if using, and refrigerate until required. — Remove the tomato tartare mix from the fridge 1 hour before serving. — To serve, spoon the tomato tartare into a serving dish. — Lay the Turkish toasts around the outside and serve.

THE DINNER PARTY

SO DELICIOUS I HAD TO SHARE IT

Tiger prawns, Campari rhubarb, finger lime

FROM THE PANTRY
Shellfish oil (Basics, page 225)

DAY BEFORE
Clean prawns and refrigerate.
Make rhubarb puree.
Prep finger limes and refrigerate.

ON THE DAY
Make red onion and
Campari base.

This is one of those 'wow' dishes that is perfect for entertaining, with a zingy, vibrant dressing of Campari and rhubarb contrasting with sweet prawns (shrimp). I've allowed two prawns per person in this recipe to work as an entrée, but if you are doing multiple courses just make it one per person.

Serve with finger bowls – it is super delicious, and you will want to get every last morsel.

PRAWNS

12 large tiger prawns (shrimp)
(U6 or U8 size, around
80–100 g/2¾–3½ oz each)

Working with one prawn at a time, place the prawn shell-side down on a cutting board, legs facing you. — Using a sharp, serrated knife, cut through the soft shell of the prawn by starting at the head. Hold the head between finger and thumb and cut through it, away from the body, splitting it open. — Turn the prawn around and continue the cut through the body to so that the prawn opens up. Cut through the flesh right to the shell but not through the shell; this is a reverse-butterflied prawn. — Rinse the head cavity under running water and remove the intestinal tract. — Place each prawn flesh-side down on the cutting board and press down with your hand to flatten. — Line a tray with paper towel and place the prawns on the tray, flesh-side down. Wrap with plastic wrap and refrigerate until required.

CAMPARI RHUBARB PUREE

250 g (9 oz) rhubarb stems,
cleaned and chopped

50 g (1¾ oz) caster (superfine) sugar

1 tablespoon Campari

juice of ½ lime

Put the chopped rhubarb into a bowl and sprinkle with the sugar. — Mix well and set aside for around 15 minutes. — Put the rhubarb in a heavy-based saucepan and add the Campari and lime juice. — Bring to a simmer, then turn the heat to the lowest setting and cook until you have a thick, dark red puree. — Stir the rhubarb often, as it will catch on the base of the pan. — Once ready, remove from the heat and set aside to cool. — Refrigerate in an airtight container until required.

CAMPARI RHUBARB AND SHELLFISH OIL

70 g (2½ oz) unsalted butter

1 tablespoon extra-virgin olive oil

2 red onions (about 150 g/5½ oz),
finely diced

2 garlic cloves, finely diced

pinch of sea salt

150 ml (5 fl oz) Campari

1 tablespoon Forvm merlot vinegar

150 g (5½ oz) Campari rhubarb
puree, as above

120 g (4½ oz) Shellfish oil
(Basics, page 225)

Heat a heavy-based saucepan over a medium heat. — Add the butter and olive oil and heat until bubbling and starting to caramelise. — Add the red onion and garlic, and sauté until soft and transparent. — Season with salt at this stage to help the mixture break down and lightly caramelise. — Deglaze the pan with the Campari and reduce, stirring, until almost all the Campari has evaporated. — Add in the merlot vinegar and rhubarb puree, stirring until combined. — Remove from the heat and whisk in the shellfish oil until you have an oily, slightly sticky, thick puree. — Set aside at room temperature.

FINGER LIMES

3 red finger limes

Cut the finger limes lengthways down the centre. — Use your thumb or a teaspoon to push out the finger lime pearls. — Check for any seeds, then refrigerate in an airtight container until required.

CHEF'S TIP
If cooking in the oven, heat
the oven to 220°C (430°F),
and preheat a roasting tray for
10 minutes. Place the prawns
shell-side down on the tray
and roast for 4–5 minutes.

TO SERVE

12 prepared tiger prawns
(shrimp), page 68

Campari, rhubarb and shellfish
oil, page 68

prepared finger limes, page 68

Heat a barbecue to hot, or alternatively use an oven (see chef's tip). — Remove the prawns from the refrigerator, unwrap and place shell-side down on a clean tray. — Spoon some of the Campari, rhubarb and shellfish oil onto the flesh and set aside for 15 minutes. — Grill the prawns shell-side down for around 3 minutes, until the flesh turns translucent. — Remove and place on a clean tray. — To serve, spoon a generous amount of the Campari, rhubarb and shellfish oil onto a large serving platter and spread out with the back of the spoon. — Dress the prawns with more Campari, rhubarb and shellfish oil. — Place the prawns on the platter, top with finger lime pearls and serve immediately.

WHEN IN DOUBT, CHOOSE RED

Negroni rigatoni

Essential red sauce
(Basics, page 216)

Fragrant chilli oil
(Basics, page 216)

DAY BEFORE
Make Negroni (page 210)
and refrigerate.

ON THE DAY
AM
Dice shallots and garlic,
grate Parmigiano Reggiano.

PM
Cook the base sauce
and set aside.

The inspiration for this dish came from that quintessential New York hot spot, Carbone, who are famous for their vodka rigatoni. I don't find that vodka adds much in terms of flavour, so I make it with my killer Negroni instead, which gives great warmth and depth of flavour.

Negroni rigatoni is always our go-to dish when we want to chill out in front of the television, and it's a knock-out dish to make for friends, too. You can use other pasta shapes if you like; it's very forgiving.

NEGRONI SAUCE

60 ml (2 fl oz) olive oil
4 shallots, finely chopped
4 garlic cloves, finely chopped
150 ml (5 fl oz) Negroni (page 210)
650 ml (22 fl oz) Essential red sauce (Basics, page 216)
1–2 tablespoons Fragrant chilli oil (Basics, page 216)

TO SERVE

sea salt
500 g (1 lb 2 oz) dried rigatoni pasta
Negroni sauce, as above
120 g (4½ oz) thickened (whipping) cream
50 g (1¾ oz) Parmigiano Reggiano, grated

In a large, wide, heavy-based saucepan or flameproof casserole dish, heat the olive oil over a medium heat. — Add the shallots and garlic and cook until softened. — Add the Negroni mix to deglaze the pan, stirring until combined. — Cook until the Negroni reduces and has almost evaporated. — Add the essential red sauce and continue to cook over a medium–low heat, stirring often, until the sauce is deep red, making sure the base of the pan doesn't scorch. — Reduce the heat to low and add the fragrant chilli oil, stirring. — Set the sauce aside until ready to serve.

Fill an 8 litre (270 fl oz) pot three-quarters full with water. — Add a good amount of sea salt and bring to a rolling boil. — Once boiling, add the rigatoni and cook according to the packet instructions (around 12–14 minutes), stirring occasionally. — Meanwhile, gently warm the Negroni sauce and bring to a simmer. — Reduce the heat and gradually add the cream to the sauce, stirring well until smooth and glossy. — Turn the heat to very low, while the pasta is cooking. — Once the pasta is nearly cooked, transfer 100 ml (3½ fl oz) of the pasta water to the Negroni sauce, stirring to combine. — Drain the cooked pasta, reserving 200 ml (7 fl oz) of the cooking water. Shake the pasta well to remove excess water. — Add the rigatoni to the sauce, gently turning until well coated. — Scatter with Parmigiano and gently fold through until it melts and is fully incorporated. — Add some of the reserved pasta water to loosen the sauce, stirring, until it is rich, creamy and smooth, evenly coating the pasta. — Season to taste and serve individually or in a bowl in the centre of the table.

CHEF'S NOTE
When you drain the pasta, remember to reserve some of the pasta water. The starches in the water help bind the pasta sauce, while at the same time lightening it.

Lamb shanks, pomegranate, charred cayenne peppers

Essential red sauce
(Basics, page 216)

Chicken stock
(Basics, page 215)

PREP AHEAD

Braise lamb shanks, prep and
store covered with sauce.

Marinate charred cayenne
peppers 2 days prior.

DAY BEFORE

Relax, go for a walk.

ON THE DAY

Warm shanks 2 hours prior and
then leave at room temperature.

This little twist on your average braised lamb shank dish will take it to another level (so much so that at our place, it's known as the Lamb Shank Redemption!).

There's richness, and spice, with a kick from the marinated chillies and an incredible acidity from the pomegranate molasses. And it's easy to prep both lamb shanks and chillies way ahead of time, and just heat through when you're ready to serve.

MARINATED CHARRED CAYENNE PEPPERS

12 cayenne peppers (long red chillies)
300 ml (10 fl oz) olive oil
2 sprigs of thyme

Place the cayenne peppers on a rack with a heatproof tray underneath, with another rack under the tray to protect the benchtop. — Use a blowtorch to sear and scorch the peppers until blackened on all sides. — Put in a bowl, cover with plastic wrap and set aside for 15 minutes. — Using a paring knife or small kitchen knife, scrape off the skin, trim off the stem, and run the knife down the side of each pepper to remove the seeds from the inside. — Place on a tray lined with paper towel and cover with more paper towel to remove excess water. — When clean and dry, put the peppers in an airtight container and cover completely with olive oil and thyme, ensuring there are no air pockets. — Refrigerate for up to 1 month.

LAMB SHANKS

1½ tablespoons olive oil
6 lamb shanks
½ teaspoon ground white pepper
1 teaspoon black peppercorns
1 teaspoon coriander seeds
1 tablespoon cumin seeds
3 red onions, peeled and diced
6 garlic cloves, minced
1 teaspoon sea salt
3 red capsicums (bell peppers), seeds and core removed, chopped
300 ml (10 fl oz) white wine (e.g. riesling)
280 g (10 oz) tomato paste (concentrated puree)
150 g (5½ oz) pomegranate molasses
zest and juice of 2 oranges
1 litre (34 fl oz) Chicken stock (Basics, page 215)
800 g (1 lb 12 oz) Essential red sauce (Basics, page 216), or substitute with 2 × 400 g (14 oz) tinned tomatoes, chopped

Heat the oven to 165°C (330°F). — Heat a 6–8 litre (203–270 fl oz) flameproof casserole dish over a medium–high heat, then add the oil. — Season the lamb shanks with white pepper and add to the pan. — Sear the shanks all over until golden, then remove and set aside. — Toast the peppercorns, coriander seeds and cumin seeds in a dry frying pan over a medium heat until fragrant. — Allow to cool, then grind in a pestle and mortar and set aside. — Using the pan you seared the shanks in (add a little extra oil if required), sauté the onions, garlic and salt over a medium heat for around 5 minutes, until caramelised. — Add the ground peppercorn, coriander and cumin mixture and sauté for 1–2 minutes. — Add the chopped capsicum and continue to sauté over a high heat for 6–8 minutes, until the capsicum caramelises and starts to break down. — Deglaze the pan with the white wine and reduce until it evaporates. — Add the tomato paste, stirring, and cook for a few minutes. — Add the pomegranate molasses and caramelise for 1–2 minutes. — Add the orange juice and zest, chicken stock and tomato sauce or tinned tomatoes and bring to a simmer. — Season with salt and black pepper. — Skim the surface as necessary, then add the lamb shanks. — Cover and braise in the oven for 2–2½ hours or until the shanks are starting to become tender, but not yet falling off the bone. — Remove the shanks from the liquid and set aside to cool.

Using a hand-held blender, blitz the braising liquid until smooth. — Pass the braising liquid though a fine sieve or strainer into a clean container, and set aside. — Once the lamb shanks are cool enough to handle, carefully remove the meat from the bone, trying to keep it in one piece. — Remove any excess fat, then put the shanks side-by-side in a roasting tray or dish. — Add the sauce to cover the shanks halfway, then cover with aluminium foil. — Cool and then refrigerate if making ahead, otherwise hold at room temperature until ready to serve.

CHEF'S TIP

The best way to prep the peppers
is with a blowtorch, otherwise
you can grill them over a high
heat on a barbecue.

If you've made the lamb shanks
days ahead, reheat them in
their sauce in the oven at 150°C
(300°F) for around 1 hour until
hot all the way through. Hold
at room temperature before
reheating as per the recipe.

TO SERVE

Lamb shanks (page 73)

braising liquid (page 73)

Marinated charred cayenne
peppers (page 73)

extra-virgin olive oil, to serve

Heat the oven to 170°C (340°F). — Bake the covered shanks for around 15 minutes. — Remove the foil, then bake the shanks for a further 5–8 minutes to brown slightly. — Remove and set aside for 5 minutes to cool. — Drain the cayenne peppers from the oil (reserve the oil for future use), place on a roasting tray, and warm in the oven for 1 minute. — Serve the shanks on a warm platter with plenty of the sauce. — Place the warmed peppers on top of the shanks, season well, and drizzle with olive oil. — Serve immediately.

'Better than hasselback' potatoes

Prep potatoes and bake.
Reheat when ready to serve.

The real hasselback potato, invented in the Hasselbacken restaurant in Stockholm, Sweden, in the 1950s, has had a renaissance over the past few years, and for good reason. By cutting the potatoes in half, then cutting slits almost all the way through and cooking them in a buttery stock and dusting them in paprika, you get a great combination of softness and crunch.

This version doubles down on the crunch by slicing the potato all the way through, then stacking the slices vertically in the baking dish – which makes an impressive sight when you take them to the table.

1.5 kg (3 lb 5 oz) kestrel potatoes (around 120 g/4½ oz) each)
150 g (5½ oz) unsalted butter
sea salt, to season
1 heaped teaspoon smoked sweet paprika

Heat the oven to 185°C (365°F), and choose a 20 cm (8 in) round ceramic pie dish. — Peel the potatoes and rinse under cold water. — Trim the ends off the potatoes to give a flat starting surface. Using a mandoline, slice each potato into rounds about 2 mm (⅛ in) thick, and divide between two large bowls, for ease of handling. — Melt the butter in a small saucepan until it begins to bubble. — Pour the melted butter over the potato slices in each bowl. Season with sea salt and toss gently until well-coated. — Start filling the pie dish with potato slices, three or four slices at a time, placed vertically, side-by-side. — Continue with the remaining slices until the pan is tightly filled. — Dust the smoked paprika over the top, then bake for 40 minutes until crisp and golden. — Remove from the oven and allow to cool for 5 minutes before serving straight from the ceramic dish at the table. — Reheat at 180°C (360°F) for 12 minutes if required.

CHEF'S TIP
It takes a bit of practice to stack the potatoes. Use one hand to hold the slices in place, pressing against the rest, and add slices in groups of three or four at a time.

Radicchio, vincotto red onion

DAY BEFORE
Prep radicchio and refrigerate.

This is a quick salad that packs a lot of flavour. It's sweet, spicy, bitter and highly colourful (a little like me), with a real style of its own. Prep the leaves in advance, then toss together to serve.

ON THE DAY
AM
Prep onion and refrigerate.

PM
Dress at the last minute, and serve.

1 head of radicchio, around 450 g (1 lb)
1 red onion, peeled
1½ tablespoons vincotto
1½ tablespoons olive oil
sea salt and freshly milled pepper

Cut the radicchio into quarters, then cut out the core that holds the leaves together. — Shred the leaves finely, rinse in iced water and spin dry in a salad spinner. — Refrigerate in an airtight container until required. — Cut the red onion in half and remove the root end. Turn the onion 90 degrees so the cut root end is facing you, then slice into thin strips. — Refrigerate in an airtight container until required. — To serve, separate the layers of onion with your fingers. Add vincotto, olive oil, sea salt and pepper and mix well together. In a large bowl, toss the radicchio and the onion mixture together until well-coated. — Transfer to a serving bowl, piling up the shredded leaves so that the salad sits high and full in the bowl, and serve immediately.

CHEF'S TIP
Cutting the onion using this technique makes it less intense in flavour, and sweeter to taste.

Raspberry, salted white chocolate

Make raspberry consommé
up to 2 weeks ahead and freeze.

DAY BEFORE
Make biscuit base.

Make jelly and hold
at room temperature.

Make salted white chocolate
mousse and flan.

ON THE DAY
Unmould flan and refrigerate.

Salted white chocolate cream has been a big dessert go-to of mine since the Sepia restaurant days, because it always makes everything better. In this simple but very tasty flan, the salt helps counteract that overly sweet flavour that white chocolate can often evoke, and lifts the dessert to the next level.

RASPBERRY CONSOMMÉ

1 kg (2 lb 3 oz) frozen raspberries	
150 g (5½ oz) pure icing (confectioners') sugar	
200 g (7 oz) raspberry liqueur (e.g. Chambord)	
150 g (5½ oz) light corn syrup	

Heat the oven to 100°C (210°F) fan-forced. If you have a steam oven, heat to 85°C (185°F) steam. — Put the frozen raspberries in a deep roasting dish and sift the sugar over the top to coat. — In a saucepan, bring the raspberry liqueur and corn syrup to a simmer. — Pour the syrup over the raspberries, then cover the tray tightly with aluminium foil. Put in the oven for around 2 hours, giving the raspberries a stir every so often. — Once the raspberries have leached all their juices, remove from the oven and immediately pass the entire mixture through a fine sieve, allowing it to drain slowly through for a few hours, at room temperature. — Once the mixture has passed through the sieve, strain the juices through a paper coffee filter for an even clearer, finer consommé. You should have at least 600 ml (20½ fl oz) raspberry consommé. — Leave to cool, then refrigerate until required. — (Note: you only need 300 ml/10 fl oz for this recipe; freeze the rest aside for another time.)

SCOTCH FINGER BASE

300 g (10½ oz) Scotch Finger biscuits or shortbread biscuits	
180 g (6½ oz) unsalted butter	
pinch of salt	

Break up the biscuits, then pulse in a food processor until you have a coarse crumb. — Meanwhile, melt the butter in a small, heavy-based saucepan over a medium heat until it begins to bubble. — Remove from the heat, add the salt and allow to cool for a minute or two. — Pour the butter into the biscuit crumbs with the food processor running and blend until incorporated. — Scrape the mixture into a bowl and set aside. — Prepare a 22 cm (8¾ in) fluted flan tin with a loose, removable base by lightly spraying with olive-oil spray, wiping lightly with paper towel to remove any excess. — Press the biscuit crumble into the base of the flan, pressing it tightly into the edges and making sure it is even. — Refrigerate until required.

RASPBERRY JELLY

300 ml (10 fl oz) Raspberry consommé, as above	
4 gelatine leaves, gold strength	

In a small pan, bring the raspberry consommé to a simmer. — Soak the gelatine in iced water for about 5 minutes, or until it becomes soft and pliable. — Squeeze out as much water as possible, then add the gelatine to the raspberry consommé, off the heat, stirring until dissolved. — Set aside at room temperature.

SALTED WHITE CHOCOLATE MOUSSE

3 gelatine leaves, gold strength	
275 g (9½ oz) Valrhona Ivoire 35% white chocolate	
600 g (1 lb 5 oz) thickened (whipping) cream	
½ teaspoon salt	

Soak the gelatine in iced water for 5 minutes until it becomes soft and pliable. — Meanwhile, break up the chocolate and put it in a heatproof bowl. — Heat 200 g (7 oz) of the cream with the salt and bring to a simmer. — Squeeze as much water from the gelatine as possible, then add the gelatine to the boiled cream, off the heat, stirring until dissolved. — Pour the boiled cream onto the chocolate one-third at a time, using a spatula to stir from the middle of the bowl to the outside until the chocolate mixture is smooth. — Allow the mixture to sit at room temperature until it has cooled to around 30°C (85°F) (about 15–20 minutes). — Meanwhile, whip the remaining 400 g (14 oz) cream to soft peaks. — Once the chocolate has cooled sufficiently, fold it through the whipped cream in batches. — Stir well to ensure there are no small lumps of cream remaining.

TO FILL THE FLAN

Place the flan tin on a cloth, then pour the white chocolate mousse onto the Scotch Finger base. — Lift the tin gently, tapping it down on the cloth once or twice to remove any excess air and help flatten the surface. — At this stage, the mixture should begin to set. If not, put it in the refrigerator. — Once the surface is firm enough, pour the raspberry jelly liquid on top. — Set in the fridge for at least 6 hours before unmoulding.

TO SERVE

To unmould the flan, use your fingers to gently pull the jelly from the sides of the mould in between the fluted edges. — Use a blowtorch very lightly around the cream area of the tin to release the base and cream. — Place the flan securely on a low platform that is smaller than the metal insert of the flan tin, such as three tins of tomatoes, so the outer case can fall away, leaving the flan stable on top of the tins. Make sure you support the mould while doing this, so that it falls away evenly and not just from one side. — Carefully lift off the metal insert of the flan tin, place on a serving plate and refrigerate for around 1 hour before serving.

CHEF'S TIP

Rather than dipping the flan tin in hot water to release the flan, which could melt the cream filling, just use a blowtorch gently around the outside, and let time and temperature do their work.

4 THE ITALIANS ARE COMING!

**CANAPES /
SNACKS**
SERVED ON ARRIVAL

Endive, bagna cauda

STARTERS
SHARED AND SERVED
AT THE SAME TIME

Seared beef, white anchovy, fennel
Crunchy beetroot, blood orange, gorgonzola

PASTA COURSE
SERVED SEPARATELY

Oxtail orzo, parmesan panko

MAINS & SIDES
SERVED TOGETHER
ON THE TABLE

King George whiting milanese
Tomatoes, peppers, burrata

DESSERT

The Italian Job: Tiramisu pannacotta
Espresso, please!

WINE TIME

Toasted almond Franciacorta style wine
Lean and dry Soave classico
Structured but juicy Tavel rosé
Earthy and Volcanic Mount Etna Sicilian red
Sweet amaro-style liqueur

COCKTAIL HOUR Hanky Panky 210

I love having our Italian friends over for dinner, because they are so passionate, fiery, loud and colourful – and so beautifully dressed. We treat each other like family; we talk about food, fashion, politics, football, and more food.

This menu is an attempt to capture that wonderful spirit and animation in a dinner party menu that everyone can enjoy.

You don't have to be Italian to want to start the night on a magnificent cocktail, or to dip crisp endive leaves into a creamy anchovy dip, scoop up finely shaved rare beef under a crunchy pile of fennel, or dig in to a rich oxtail ragu with risoni pasta under a breadcrumb crust.

In fact, it might help if your guests aren't Italian at all – my Italian friends always protest when I add a twist to a traditional recipe. So of course, I'm going to do that deliberately here, just to rile them.

The truth is that the bedrock of Italian cuisine is so rich and so deep, you can imagine it in a million different ways to create something new and exciting and it will still taste, sound and look Italian.

You can pluck a technique from a specific region or city, such as 'a la milanese' from Milan, which denotes a dish fried in a golden sheath of breadcrumbs – and then apply it to one of Australia's finest, most delicate fish, the King George whiting. It's not traditional, but it respects the past while simultaneously upending it.

I know that even when my Italian friends pretend to tear their hair out at the fact that I have combined the very best of both tiramisu and panna cotta into one stupendous tiramisu panna cotta mousse cake, they're secretly enjoying themselves – and they always ask for seconds.

Be warned, if this menu works the way I think it will, you will find yourself making espresso coffees at 1 am, because by then, everyone will think they're Italian.

THE PLAYLIST **CHARLOTTE GAINSBOURG** IRM **THE CHEMICAL BROTHERS** Surrend Collected **MALCOLM MCLAREN AND THE BOOTZILLA ORCHESTRA** Waltz Darlin Strangers in the Night **THE FLAMINGOS** I Only Have Eyes for You **LUDOVICO EINAU**

IGARETTES AFTER SEX Cigarettes After Sex **LAMB** Lamb **MASSIVE ATTACK** **TTA JAMES** Tell Mama **DINAH WASHINGTON** Dinah '62 **FRANK SINATRA** lands **OTIS REDDING** The Soul Album

Endive*, bagna cauda

DAY BEFORE
Prep endive and refrigerate.

ON THE DAY
AM
Make bagna cauda and keep
at room temperature, covered.

Originating from the Northern Italian region of Piedmont, Bagna cauda literally means 'hot bath' in the local dialect, in that it's a hot bath of garlic and anchovy in which you dip crisp raw vegetables. It's often enjoyed on Christmas Eve as part of a family celebration, but it's also a great dinner party dish at any time of the year, with built-in interactive fun.

It needs to be served warm, so make sure you heat both the sauce and the serving dish just before serving. Traditionally it is served with artichoke leaves and bread, but I really love the bitterness of endive leaves, which also make the perfect scoop – so long as there are no double-dippers!

ENDIVE

4 heads of endive
(chicory/Belgian endive)

Separate the leaves individually and select the nice, even middle leaves. (Reserve the other leaves to use another time.) — Put in a container lined with damp paper towel, cover with more damp paper towel, then cover and refrigerate until required.

BAGNA CAUDA

5 garlic cloves (about 30 g/1 oz)

12 anchovy fillets (e.g. Ortiz), drained of oil and chopped

100 g (3½ oz) butter, softened

100 ml (3½ fl oz) olive oil

Using a microplane, grate the garlic into a bowl. — Add the chopped anchovies and mix together with a spatula. — Add the softened butter and use the spatula to cream the ingredients together. — Pour in the olive oil gradually, in three batches, and beat using the spatula until incorporated. — Pour into a small, heavy-based saucepan and cook over a low heat for around 8 minutes, allowing the anchovy to break down and melt, and the garlic to gently poach in the oil, rather than roast. — The mixture will split, so just keep whisking it together again as it cooks. — Remove from the heat and allow to cool for a few minutes. — Set aside until ready to serve.

TO SERVE

70 g (2½ oz) mascarpone cheese

Warm the anchovy and garlic mixture in a saucepan until it reaches around 70°C (160°F). — Whisk in the mascarpone and then blitz with a hand-held blender until incorporated. — Pour into a warm bowl, and put this in the centre of a larger bowl. — Arrange the endive leaves around the bagna cauda and serve.

CHEF'S TIP
The mixture will look split, and technically it is, but the magic is in getting both the oil and the thicker mixture at the bottom when you dip. Delicious!

*Witlof (chicory/Belgian endive) or curly endive.

Seared beef, white anchovy, fennel

A play on the idea of the classic beef carpaccio, this is a great sharing dish for the centre of the table. The dressing of boquerones (pickled white anchovies) slightly pickles the beef, and the freshness of shaved fennel lifts it to the next level.

DAY BEFORE
Air-dry beef for 12 hours prior.
Make dressing and refrigerate.

ON THE DAY
AM
Sear beef, slice fennel.

PM
Slice beef and refrigerate.

SEARED BEEF

450 g (1 lb) centre-cut beef tenderloin, trimmed

10 ml (¼ fl oz) extra-virgin olive oil, plus extra for searing

ground white pepper

sea salt

Purchase the beef and wrap in paper towel 2 days prior to serving. Change the paper towel every 12 hours. — Leave the beef on a rack in the refrigerator for 12 hours prior to serving, to air dry. — Place the beef on a tray and rub all over with olive oil. — Season evenly with white pepper. — Heat a heavy frying pan over a medium heat and add a little extra olive oil. — Once the oil starts to smoke, sear the tenderloin on all sides by rolling it around in the pan, giving a good, even crust. — Remove to a clean tray and season with sea salt. — Wrap the beef tightly in plastic wrap, while still warm, to form a cylindrical shape. — Refrigerate for at least 2 hours, to help firm the meat. — Prior to slicing, put the beef in the freezer for around 25 minutes. — Cut several 20 × 30 cm (8 × 12 in) sheets of baking paper. Lightly spray one side of each sheet with oil, and set aside. — Once the outside of the beef feels firm, remove the plastic wrap. — Using a sharp knife, cut the beef as finely as you can, and place the slices on the oiled baking paper in a single layer, without overlapping. — Once one sheet is covered, place another sheet on top and continue until you have around 18 thin slices of beef. — Wrap in plastic wrap and refrigerate until required.

SHAVED FENNEL

1 baby fennel

Fill a container with ice and water and refrigerate until very cold. — Cut the fennel in half lengthways. Using a mandoline, finely shave each half-fennel on the cut side — Immediately submerge the fennel in the iced water. — Cover and refrigerate. — Around 2 hours prior to serving, drain the fennel well, then spin it in a salad spinner to remove any excess water. — Store in an airtight container lined with paper towel and refrigerate until required.

WHITE ANCHOVY DRESSING

50 g (1¾ oz) white anchovies (boquerones), e.g. Ortiz

zest of 1 lemon

30 ml (1 fl oz) lemon juice

1½ teaspoons caster (superfine) sugar

½ teaspoon light soy sauce

30 ml (1 fl oz) extra-virgin olive oil

Drain the anchovies on paper towel to remove the excess oil, then cut into small pieces and set aside. — In a bowl, combine the lemon zest and juice, sugar and soy sauce, and mix until the sugar is dissolved. Whisk in the oil. — Pour the dressing over the anchovies, and refrigerate until required.

TO SERVE

Seared beef, as above

White anchovy dressing at room temperature, as above

Shaved fennel, as above

Remove the sliced beef from the refrigerator and, using a small palette knife, place individual slices onto a large sharing platter, slightly overlapping. — Mix the anchovy dressing once again and spoon over the beef until well coated, ensuring the anchovy is evenly distributed. — Arrange the shaved fennel over the beef. Serve immediately.

THE DINNER PARTY

Crunchy beetroot, blood orange, gorgonzola

FROM THE PANTRY
Seasoned rice-wine vinegar
(Basics, page 224)

DAY BEFORE
Prep blood orange.

ON THE DAY
Prep the beetroot and make
the blood orange dressing.

This is such a delicious salad, and one I think you will make time and again. It's almost crunchy with raw beetroot, creamy with gorgonzola and fragrant with walnut oil, and it looks amazing. If blood oranges are not in season, use navel or valencia oranges

BLOOD ORANGES

3 blood oranges or 2 navel oranges, around 500 g (1 lb 2 oz)

Zest the oranges and set the zest aside. — To remove the peel from the oranges, first trim off the tops and bottoms. — Stand each orange upright, and use a small, serrated knife to cut from top to bottom, following the natural curve of the orange, removing the peel and all the white pith in one go. — Cut the oranges into even slices around ½ cm (¼ in) thick. — Store in an airtight container and refrigerate until required.

BLOOD ORANGE AND WALNUT DRESSING

40 ml (1¼ fl oz) Seasoned rice-wine vinegar (Basics, page 224)

zest and juice of 1 blood orange (about 40 ml/1¼ fl oz juice)

40 ml (1¼ fl oz) extra-virgin olive oil

2 teaspoons walnut oil (e.g. LeBlanc)

In a bowl, mix the seasoned rice-wine vinegar, blood orange zest and juice until combined. — Whisk in the olive oil and walnut oil, then hold at room temperature until required.

BEETROOT MATCHSTICKS

1 or 2 large, firm beetroot (beets), around 350 g (12½ oz)

Wearing protective gloves to keep the beetroot from staining your hands, peel the beetroots then trim their tops and tails. — Using a mandoline, slice the beetroot 3–4 mm (⅛ in) thick. — Put the slices in stacks, then cut into matchstick lengths (you can use the julienne blade of the mandoline for this). — Stack the matchsticks neatly in an airtight container and refrigerate until required.

TO SERVE

100 g (3½ oz) gorgonzola dolce

blood orange slices, as above

Blood orange and walnut dressing, as above

Beetroot matchsticks, as above

On a large plate with a high rim, break up pieces of the gorgonzola and spread out over the base. — Arrange the orange slices on top of the gorgonzola. — Spoon some blood orange and walnut dressing over the oranges. — Put the beetroot matchsticks in a large bowl, trying to ensure they are all lying in the same direction. Season the beetroot with salt and pepper, then spoon over some of the blood orange and walnut dressing. — Using tongs, or your hands (wear protective gloves), gently turn the beetroot in the dressing until coated, then lay over the blood orange. It looks quite dramatic if you keep the matchsticks all lying in the same direction. — Spoon over a little extra dressing and serve.

CHEF'S TIP
Storing the beetroot matchsticks all pointing in one direction, rather than tossed together, will make them easier to plate. The larger the beetroot, the longer the matchsticks will be.

Oxtail orzo, parmesan panko

FROM THE PANTRY
Essential red sauce
(Basics, page 216)
Fragrant chilli oil
(Basics, page 216)

DAY BEFORE
Braise oxtail, remove from bone.
Make oxtail sauce.

ON THE DAY
Prep the crumbs and parmesan.
Cook orzo and refrigerate.

A good recipe will never die, but it will be born again in many different ways as it evolves over time. This much-loved dish from my restaurant Sepia started with spanner crab, and used buckwheat instead of rice. Then I moved on to using ox cheek, short ribs and brisket, and adopted orzo as well.

Orzo (along with its cousin, risoni) is a rice-shaped pasta that absorbs the flavour of whatever it is in, from minestrone soup to a hearty braise. This recipe is like a cross between a risotto and a rich stew, lightened by the orzo. Once you have made it, feel free to adapt and evolve it yourself.

BRAISED OXTAIL

2 kg (4 lb 6 oz) grain-fed oxtail, cut into sections	
1 teaspoon ground white pepper	
50 g (1¾ oz) vegetable oil	
2 onions, peeled and cut into quarters	
3 medium carrots, peeled	
2 celery stalks	
6 garlic cloves, lightly crushed	
10 black peppercorns	
5 cloves	
½ bunch (20 g/¾ oz) thyme	
2 bay leaves	
200 ml (7 fl oz) Japanese light soy sauce	
200 ml (7 fl oz) mirin	
200 ml (7 fl oz) tawny port	
3 litres (101 fl oz) water	

YIELDS 600 G (1 LB 5 OZ) COOKED MEAT AND 2.5 LITRES (85 FL OZ) BROTH

Refrigerate the oxtail on paper towel for 2 hours prior to cooking, if possible, to ensure it is dry and free of blood. — Heat a heavy-based 6–8 litre (203–270 fl oz) pot over a medium–high heat. — Lay the oxtail on a tray and dust all over with the white pepper. — Add the oil to the pot and, when hot, add the oxtail in two to three batches, roasting on all sides until golden and well-sealed. — Remove from the pot, and drain off the excess oil. — Return the oxtail to the pot along with the remaining ingredients; the oxtail should be covered. — Bring to a simmer, skimming off the fat and impurities with a small ladle. — As you skim the surface, add more water (up to 500 ml/17 fl oz) to ensure the oxtail remains covered. — Braise over a low heat for around 3 hours, skimming frequently and topping up with water as required. — Once the oxtail is tender and the meat comes away from the bone, use a kitchen spider or slotted spoon to remove the oxtail from the stock. — Remove the vegetables and discard, then strain the broth through a sieve lined with a paper filter, into a clean bowl. — Once the oxtail is cool enough to handle, pick off the lobes of meat, trying not to break it up too much, and discard the fat and bones. — Put the meat in a container, cover with the broth, and cool completely. — Once cool, cover and refrigerate for up to 3 days, or if making far in advance, freeze the oxtail in the broth.

OXTAIL SAUCE

50 g (1¾ oz) butter	
1 teaspoon Korean chilli flakes (gochugaru)	
600 g (1 lb 5 oz) braised oxtail, as above	
400 g (14 oz) Essential red sauce (Basics, page 216) or tinned chopped tomatoes	
250 ml (8½ fl oz) oxtail broth	

In a heavy-based pot, melt the butter over a medium heat. — Add the chilli flakes and sauté for a few seconds until aromatic. — Add the oxtail meat, stirring until coated, then add the red sauce or tomatoes and the broth. — Bring to a simmer, and allow to reduce until thickened. — Season to taste.

PARMESAN PANKO CRUMB

30 g (1 oz) unsalted butter	
2 garlic cloves, cut in half	
1 tablespoon thyme leaves	
80 g (2¾ oz) panko crumbs	
25 g (1 oz) Parmigiano Reggiano, grated	
2 tablespoons parsley leaves, chopped	

Heat a frying pan over a medium heat. — Add the butter and stir until melted. — Once the butter starts to bubble, add the garlic and cook slowly, without colouring. — Add the thyme leaves, stirring. — Once fragrant, add the panko crumbs and stir until well-coated. — Continue to cook gently until the crumbs turn a golden brown. — Remove from the heat and pour into a heatproof bowl. — Pick out the garlic halves and discard, then leave the crumbs to cool slightly. — Add the parmesan and parsley, tossing to mix. — Spoon into an airtight container and set aside at room temperature until required.

ORZO PASTA

1 heaped tablespoon sea salt	
250 g (9 oz) orzo pasta or risoni	

In a large, heavy-based pot, bring 4 litres (135 fl oz) of water to the boil. — Add the salt and bring the water back to a rolling boil. — Stir the water and then rain in the pasta; this will help separate the grains. — Bring to the boil and simmer for around 7 minutes, or until al dente. — Strain through a colander and rinse the pasta under cold running water to cool completely. — Drain well and set aside until required. — If cooked in advance, store in an airtight container in the refrigerator.

TO SERVE

Braised oxtail (page 93)
Oxtail sauce (page 93)
Orzo pasta, as above
1 tablespoon butter
Fragrant chilli oil (Basics, page 216) (optional)
Parmesan panko crumbs (page 93)
150 g (5½ oz) mascarpone cheese

Warm the oxtail in a large, heavy-based saucepan. — When ready to serve, heat the orzo in boiling water for a couple of seconds, then drain well. — Add the orzo to the oxtail and stir through until well distributed. — Add the butter, stirring, and taste for seasoning. — Divide into warm pasta bowls and drizzle with chilli oil, if using. — Scatter with the toasted panko crumbs. — Serve immediately with creamy mascarpone on the side.

CHEF'S TIP

I suggest you choose grain-fed beef, as it has a higher fat content that will give a more luxurious finish. You can swap the oxtail for beef cheek, using the same recipe.

A GOOD RECIPE EVOLVES OVER TIME

King George whiting milanese

FROM THE PANTRY

Clarified butter if pan-frying
(Basics, page 215)

Salmoriglio (Basics, page 224)

DAY BEFORE

Prep the fish.

ON THE DAY

Crumb the fish.

Caught off the south coast of Australia, all the way from Western Australia to Victoria, King George whiting is a sustainable species that reproduces quickly and is proving resilient to fishing practices. I absolutely love it because it's so delicate and firm-fleshed, and very clean and sweet-tasting.

It's a very versatile fish, something I want to showcase here by using two different methods of achieving a crisp crumb coating. You can either pan-fry it in clarified butter for a rich, buttery flavour, or deep-fry, for a super-crisp result.

TO CRUMB THE FISH

6 × 100 g (3½ oz) King George whiting fillets

2 sprigs rosemary, picked

½ bunch lemon thyme (20 g/¾ oz), picked

150 g (5½ oz) panko crumbs

60 g (2 oz) rice flour or plain (all-purpose) flour

1 teaspoon salt

1 teaspoon Aleppo chilli flakes

2 eggs

Place the fillets skin-side down on a board, and lightly wipe the flesh with paper towel to remove any scale or residue. — Using fish pliers, remove the pin bones from each fillet and discard. — Using a sharp filleting knife, remove the skin from each fillet, starting at the tail end and running it between skin and flesh, pulling gently on the skin and wriggling the knife at the same time to separate it. — Place the fillets on a tray lined with paper towel and refrigerate for at least 3 hours. — Finely chop the rosemary. — Chop the thyme, not quite as finely, then mix the two herbs with the panko crumbs and set aside. — Place the flour on a tray. Add the salt and Aleppo chilli flakes, mix well and set aside. — Crack the eggs into a bowl, whisk in 1 tablespoon of water and set aside. — Following this order, place the fish fillets, seasoned flour, egg wash and herbed panko crumbs on a bench from left to right, with a clean tray at the end. — Holding the fish fillet by the tail end, dredge it in the flour and dust off the excess. — Next, dip it into the egg wash and run it against the edges of the bowl to remove the excess. — Lastly, place it on the herbed panko crumbs and coat well, pressing the crumbs against the fish, then place the crumbed fillet on the clean tray. — Repeat with the remaining fillets, then refrigerate until required.

TO PAN-FRY THE FISH

150 g (5½ oz) Clarified butter (Basics, page 215)

salt

Preheat the oven to 80°C (175°F). — Place a wire rack on a tray, line it with paper towel and warm it in the oven. — Heat a large non-stick frying pan over a medium heat, then add one-third of the clarified butter. — When hot, put two crumbed fillets in the butter at a time and fry for around 1 minute, until golden. — Gently turn and cook for a further minute before transferring to the paper-lined rack in the oven. — Season with salt and keep warm. — Repeat with the remaining fillets.

TO DEEP-FRY THE FISH

2 litres (68 fl oz) canola oil

sea salt

Heat the oven to 80°C (175°F). — Place a wire rack on a tray, line it with paper towel and warm it in the oven. — Heat the oil to 190°C (375°F) in a heavy-based 8 litre (270 fl oz) pot or deep-fryer. — Deep-dry two crumbed fillets at a time for around 1–2 minutes, until golden and crisp. — Drain well, season with sea salt then place on the paper-lined wire rack in the oven to keep warm. — Repeat with the remaining fillets.

CHEF'S TIP

It takes two people to crumb fish like a pro. The first person should flour and egg-wash each fillet, then place it onto the crumbs. The second person then coats the fish in crumbs and places it on a tray. Otherwise, it gets a bit messy, and you can make the crumb soft with too much egg-wash.

TO SERVE

200 g (7 oz) Salmoriglio dressing (Basics, page 224)

Pour half the salmoriglio sauce onto the base of a high-sided plate. — Place the fried King George whiting on top of the salmoriglio sauce. — Serve the remaining sauce in a bowl on the side.

Tomatoes, peppers, burrata

FROM THE PANTRY
Marinated bullhorn peppers
(Basics, page 219)

ON THE DAY
Prep tomatoes, and remove
burrata from refrigerator
15 minutes prior.

Based loosely on Italy's Caprese salad, this is a wonderful twist using roasted bullhorn (romano) peppers, cherry tomatoes and creamy burrata cheese, drenched in olive oil. Marinating the tomatoes beforehand means the salt draws out the natural sugars, giving you the most amazing dressing. Might pay to have some crusty bread nearby, to help mop up it up.

PEPPERS AND TOMATOES

300 g (10½ oz) cherry tomatoes
or tear-drop cherry tomatoes

sea salt and pepper

1 tablespoon Forvm cabernet
sauvignon or red-wine vinegar

60 ml (2 fl oz) olive oil

180 g (6½ oz) Marinated bullhorn
peppers (Basics, page 219) or
Navarrico piquillo roasted peppers

1 fresh burrata cheese

Prepare the tomatoes at least 30 minutes prior to serving. Cut them in half, season well with sea salt and pepper, then drizzle with the vinegar and half the olive oil. — Gently stir together and set aside at room temperature. — Cut the marinated bullhorn peppers into 5 mm (¼ in) dice and set aside. — Remove the burrata from the refrigerator, drain on paper towel and leave at room temperature for 15 minutes. — To serve, combine the roasted bullhorn peppers and marinated cherry tomatoes, mixing well. — Spoon onto the serving plate and spread out evenly. — Pour the remaining olive oil over the top. — Arrange the burrata in the centre and serve immediately.

CHEF'S TIP
Bring the burrata out of the
refrigerator 15 minutes prior
and rest on kitchen paper.

This will stop excess water
running form the burrata when
served and allows the cheese
to warm slightly so that it's not
fridge cold.

The Italian job: tiramisu pannacotta

PREP AHEAD
Make the mousse cake up
to 2 days prior.

DAY BEFORE
Make praline, and unmould
mousse cake.
Make coffee caramel.

When you can't decide between two great Italian desserts – tiramisu and pannacotta – why not roll them both into one?!

Taking elements from both tiramisu and pannacotta threw my Italian guests into a tizz, as they shook their heads and cried *'Mamma mia, Martino, mi raccomando!'* They thought I had lost the plot and committed gastronomic blasphemy, but I knew it would be sensational. How could it not?

I use a 6 cup (18 × 9 cm/7 × 3½ in high) bundt tin for its decorative shape, but you could also serve this in individual glasses for a bit of fun. If you make it a few days ahead, you can unmould it the day before, so there's no stress at the time of serving.

CUSTARD BASE

5 egg yolks	
120 g (4½ oz) condensed milk	
120 g (4½ oz) evaporated milk	
200 ml (7 fl oz) full-cream (whole) milk	
1 teaspoon vanilla paste	

Whisk the egg yolks in a bowl and set aside. — Pour the remaining ingredients into a saucepan and bring to a simmer, stirring. — Pour the milk over the egg yolks, whisking constantly until well combined. — Pour the egg mixture back into the pan, making sure the yolks have been fully incorporated. — Heat gently and stir continuously while bringing the temperature to 82°C (180°F) – do not boil or overheat. — Remove from the heat, strain through a fine sieve into a clean bowl, then set aside.

COFFEE SOAK

120 g (4½ oz) espresso coffee	
25 ml (¾ fl oz) Frangelico	

Mix the coffee and Frangelico in a bowl and set aside.

THREE-MILK PANNACOTTA

9 gelatine leaves, gold strength	
400 g (14 oz) Custard base, as above	
200 g (7 oz) Valrhona 32% Blond Dulcey chocolate	
50 ml (1¾ fl oz) Frangelico	
pinch of sea salt	
400 g (14 oz) whipped cream	
8 or 9 savoiardi (lady fingers), trimmed to 6cm/2½ in long	
Coffee soak, as above	

Spray a decorative bundt tin with olive-oil spray, then wipe with paper towel and spray the inside again, lightly, without wiping it off. — Soak the gelatine leaves in a bowl of iced water for around 5 minutes, to hydrate. — Pour the custard base into a saucepan and warm to around 50°C (120°F), stirring constantly, then remove from the heat. — Squeeze out the excess water from the gelatine leaves then add them to the custard mixture, stirring until incorporated. — Melt the Dulcey chocolate in the microwave until fluid, then stir through the custard mix until fully incorporated. — Add the Frangelico and sea salt, stirring to incorporate. — Cool the mixture to 35°C (95°F), then gently fold in the whipped cream in three batches, trying not to lose much air from the mixture. — Pour the mixture into the prepared mould, filling to within 1 cm (½ in) from the top. — Tap down the mould on a cloth to remove excess air and to flatten the surface, and then set aside at room temperature. — Working quickly, one savoiardi biscuit at a time, dip the biscuit into the coffee soak, then remove and tap to drain. — Insert the end of the biscuit into the mould with the mousse, pushing it down not quite to the bottom of the mousse, making sure it stands up. — Repeat with the remaining savoiardi biscuits, working your way around the mould, and separating them evenly. It's okay if they stick out the top of the mousse slightly. — Cover the surface with baking paper, then refrigerate overnight to set. — The next day, leave the mousse cake at room temperature for 20 minutes before unmoulding. — Use your fingers to loosen the mousse from the mould, then turn it upside down onto a serving plate. It will take time to fall out. If it needs help, use the warmth from your hands on the outside of the mould, or use a blowtorch on the lowest setting to warm the mould. — Once turned out, cover and refrigerate until required.

HAZELNUT PRALINE

160 g (5½ oz) hazelnuts

200 g (7 oz) caster (superfine) sugar

pinch of sea salt

Heat the oven to 180°C (360°F). — Pour the hazelnuts onto a tray and dry-roast in the oven for 16 minutes, shaking occasionally. — Remove and set aside until cool enough to handle. — Line a bowl with a tea towel (dish towel), then pour in the hazelnuts. Using the tea towel, rub the hazelnuts together to remove the skins. — Set the cleaned hazelnuts aside and discard the skins. — Line a large tray with baking paper and set to one side. — To make a dry caramel, heat a heavy-based saucepan over a medium heat. — Add one-third of the sugar in an even layer in the pan. — Once the sugar starts to melt, turn down the heat and allow the sugar to become liquid. — Add another third of the caster sugar on top of the liquid sugar, and swirl until evenly spread, allowing this to melt into the liquid sugar. — Lastly, add the remaining sugar and repeat the process until all sugar has melted into a rich, dark caramel. You can turn up the heat to caramelise the sugar more, but be careful not to burn it, or it will be bitter. — Add the roasted hazelnuts and sea salt and use a rubber spatula to coat the nuts in the caramel. — Pour the praline mixture onto the lined tray, allowing it to spread out and cool completely. — Once hardened, break it up into pieces and store in an airtight container at room temperature.

COFFEE CARAMEL

50 g (1¾ oz) liquid glucose

250 g (9 oz) caster (superfine) sugar

350 g (12½ oz) thickened (whipping) cream

30 ml (1 fl oz) espresso coffee

30 ml (1 fl oz) Frangelico

50 g (1¾ oz) butter, diced

pinch of salt

Pour the glucose into a heavy-based pan and warm over a medium heat. — When melted and fluid, sprinkle in one-third of the sugar and turn the heat to medium–high. — Once the sugar starts to melt, turn down the heat and allow the sugar to become liquid. — Add another third of the caster sugar on top of the liquid sugar, and swirl until evenly spread, allowing this to melt into the liquid sugar. — Lastly, add the remaining sugar and repeat the process until all sugar has melted into a rich, dark caramel. — At this stage, add in the cream – do this carefully, as it will create steam and bubble up. — Add the coffee and Frangelico, and bring to the boil. — Simmer for 1 minute, then remove from the heat. — Allow to cool for a few minutes, then whisk in the butter and season with the salt. — Leave to cool at room temperature – there's no need to refrigerate.

TO SERVE

Mousse cake, page 101

Hazelnut praline, as above

Coffee caramel, as above

Put the praline in a clean tea towel (dish towel), wrap it up, and use a rolling pin to smash it into small pieces. — Scatter the crushed praline in the centre of the mousse cake. — When ready to serve, pour the coffee caramel over the cake.

CHEF'S TIP

The praline can be as fine or as coarse as you like. I prefer larger chunks and shards, which creates an amazing textural contrast with the softness of the mousse cake.

5 FAMILY KNOWS BEST

ALL DISHES
SERVED TOGETHER
ON THE TABLE AS
A FEAST

Garlic mozzarella pull-apart
Roasted salmon, miso dill butter
Foolproof braised chicken, capers, olives
Chicken fat rice
Creamed sweetcorn, lime butter
Broccolini, preserved lemon, macadamia

DESSERT

Lisbon chocolate cake

WINE TIME

Vintage Champagne (*served in white wine glasses*)
Savoury Rhône Valley white blend
Margaret River chardonnay (*best to carafe wine before serving*)
Cool-climate Tasmanian pinot noir
Sweet Madeira-style wine

COCKTAIL HOUR Gimlet 211

When you're cooking for family, it's nice to reference things that you all experienced together, growing up. Everyone will have developed their own tastes since then, but the memories are shared. Think of your own memories, and whether they are triggered by the smell of Nana's chicken noodle soup, or the warm spices of a curry, or the sweet, soft crumb of a cake. Even if your family had very little, these memories will be special, and make you smile.

The idea of this menu is to feed the family in a way that brings everyone together – including you. Having everything prepped and ready to go will mean you can join in the family fun without having to rush off to the kitchen all the time.

Variety and choice are more important here than ego-driven experimentation – besides, families are very good at taking down the high and mighty – so we're going to cover the table with fish, meat and vegetables and make sure there's something for everyone, young and old. That doesn't mean it will be over in a flash, it just means everyone can relax and eat as much or as little as they like.

The pull-apart loaf is a fun way to 'break bread' together, and goes perfectly with everything else on the table. Roasted salmon is so easy to do, and richly rewarding to eat; and the braised chicken dish is classic comfort food, elevated to the next level. Vegetable dishes star in their own right here, with simple but effective accompaniments.

My last piece of advice is to make a big, beautiful cake for dessert to place in the centre of the table. It's so celebratory, and will remind family members of their childhood birthday cakes. Plus, the leftovers can be packed up and taken home to be enjoyed the next day.

p with Donald Byrd **MARVIN GAYE** What's Going On **JAMES BLAKE** Covers EP
ı Monde **RYUICHI SAKAMOTO** Music for Film **CURTIS MAYFIELD** Move on Up

Garlic mozzarella pull-apart

You can't get much more family-friendly than this garlicky, cheesy, pull-apart loaf. And the best thing is, you don't have to make and prove the dough; just use an everyday loaf. Get it prepped and into the freezer and then you can bake it from frozen on the day.

FROM THE PANTRY
Roasted garlic butter
(Basics, page 223)

PREP AHEAD
Make roasted garlic butter,
fill loaf and freeze.

ON THE DAY
Bake 1 hour prior,
then keep warm.

TO MAKE THE LOAF

1 × 700 g (1 lb 9 oz) soft white loaf, thickly sliced

340 g (12 oz) Roasted garlic butter (Basics, page 223)

300 g (10½ oz) mozzarella, grated

Remove all the crusts from the bread, and lay the slices out on the benchtop. — Spread each slice with an even layer of garlic butter, then scatter with grated mozzarella. — Lay out a length of plastic wrap, around 40 × 50 cm (15¾ × 19¾ in). — Stack each slice on top of each other, reversing the last slices so that the plain side is on the outside, and press lightly together. — Wrap the loaf in the plastic wrap so that it holds the shape of a loaf, and press it into a 22 × 12 × 7 cm (8¾ × 4¾ × 2¾ in) deep loaf tin. — Freeze for up to a week before using.

TO BAKE THE LOAF

2 tablespoons butter, softened

sea salt and pepper

Heat the oven to 180°C (360°F). — Remove bread from the freezer (don't thaw it; you can bake it from frozen). Unwrap the loaf and discard the plastic wrap. — Lightly brush the loaf tin with butter and season with salt and pepper, then return the bread to the tin. — Cover with aluminium foil and bake for 20 minutes. — Remove the foil, then bake for a further 20 minutes or until the top is crisp and golden brown and the cheese has melted. — Remove from the oven and keep warm. — To serve, remove from the tin and put in the centre of the table for people to help themselves.

Roasted salmon, miso dill butter

PREP AHEAD
Make the mustard, miso and dill butter and refrigerate or freeze.

DAY BEFORE
Prep watercress, pea sprouts and chives.

Clean and pin-bone salmon and refrigerate.

ON THE DAY
Salt and rinse the salmon.

Spread with butter and refrigerate.

An impressive share dish to place in the centre of the family table, this can be prepared in advance and simply baked and served – too easy. The grain mustard, miso and dill butter is a great contrast with the richness of the salmon. Earmark it for future use, too – it's great with other seafood and shellfish, and even with grilled vegetables. And don't forget the salad; it not only brings a new level of freshness, it makes the dish look amazing, too.

MUSTARD, MISO AND DILL BUTTER

250 g (9 oz) unsalted butter, softened

130 g (4½ oz) white miso paste (preferably saikyo miso)

1½ tablespoons light soy sauce

1½ tablespoons mirin

1½ tablespoons lemon juice

pinch of cayenne pepper

zest of 1 lemon

50 g (1¾ oz) grain mustard

30 g (1 oz) Dijon mustard

40 g (1½ oz/about 1 bunch) dill, leaves picked and chopped

MAKES 520 G (1 LB 2 OZ)

Add the softened butter to the bowl of a stand mixer. — Beat on high using the paddle attachment until light and fluffy, scraping down the sides every so often. — Once the butter is light and airy, add the miso and continue to beat until well incorporated. — Mix the soy, mirin and lemon juice together in a bowl, then slowly stream the mixture into the butter while beating, until well incorporated. — Add cayenne pepper, lemon zest, grain mustard and Dijon mustard and beat until incorporated. — Add the dill and fold in with a spatula. — Scrape the butter into an airtight container and set aside, or refrigerate if making in advance.

SALAD GREENS

60 g (2 oz/about 1 bunch) watercress, picked

40 g (1½ oz/about 2 bunches) pea shoots

20 g (¾ oz/about 1 bunch) chives, snipped into 5 cm (2 in) batons

Put the watercress, pea shoots and chives in a bowl of iced water and refrigerate for 1 hour to refresh. — Drain, then spin in a salad spinner to remove the excess water. — Refrigerate in an airtight container lined with paper towel until required.

TO PREPARE THE SALMON

1 kg (2 lb 3 oz) salmon fillet, cut from the centre, skin-on, pin bones removed

50 g (1¾ oz) sea salt flakes

2 level tablespoons sugar

Make sure the salmon is free of scales and bones. — Place on a tray, skin-side up. — Mix the sea salt flakes and sugar in a bowl. Scatter half the mixture over the salmon skin, then turn the fish over and scatter the flesh side with the remaining mixture, ensuring an even coating. — Leave for 30 minutes, for the fish to lightly cure. — Rinse the salmon in a bowl of iced water and pat dry with paper towel. — Refrigerate until ready to use.

TO ROAST THE SALMON

salmon fillet, as above

sea salt and freshly milled black pepper

Mustard, miso and dill butter, as above, softened to room temperature

salad greens, as above

3 teaspoons lemon juice

1 tablespoon olive oil

Heat the oven to 190°C (375°F). — Line a roasting tin with baking paper. — Season the salmon all over with salt and pepper, then place skin-side down onto the paper. — Using a palette knife, spread the mustard, miso and dill butter all over the flesh until well-coated. — Bake for 15–18 minutes, until the butter has melted and caramelised, and the salmon is just pink. — Rest for 3–4 minutes, then use the baking paper to lift the salmon from the tin and slide it onto a serving plate. — Put the salad greens in a bowl and dress with the lemon juice, olive oil, salt and pepper. — Arrange the salad over the salmon and serve immediately.

Foolproof braised chicken, capers, olives

FROM THE PANTRY
Chicken stock
(Basics, page 215)

Green sauce forever
(Basics, page 217)

I'm calling this foolproof because it's easy to throw together, and very forgiving – you can inadvertently overcook it and the chicken will still be deliciously juicy. You can even braise the chicken a few hours earlier and leave it at room temperature, then reheat for 15 minutes in the oven at 180°C (360°F). Plus, I've never met anyone who didn't love it.

DAY BEFORE
Trim the chicken and make the braising liquid.

CHICKEN

| 6 large chicken thighs, 200 g (7 oz) each (skin on, bone in) |
| 250 ml (8½ fl oz) Chicken stock (Basics, page 215) |
| 180 ml (6 fl oz) white wine (e.g. riesling) |
| 60 ml (2 fl oz) mirin |
| 30 ml (1 fl oz) light soy sauce |
| 200 g (7 oz) kalamata olives, drained and 50 ml (1¾ fl oz) brine reserved |
| 50 g (1¾ oz) salted capers, rinsed |
| 8 garlic cloves, peeled and lightly crushed |
| 1 tablespoon dried oregano |
| 2 tablespoons fresh thyme leaves |
| ½ teaspoon chilli flakes, mild |
| 2 bay leaves |
| 150 ml (5 fl oz) olive oil |
| sea salt and pepper |
| 1 tablespoon sweet smoked paprika |
| fresh picked oregano, to serve |
| 1 batch Green sauce forever (Basics, page 217) |

Heat the oven to 200°C (390°F). — Trim any excess fat from the chicken thighs, then arrange in a roasting dish so they fit snugly. — In a bowl, combine the chicken stock, wine, mirin, soy sauce, olive brine, olives, capers, garlic, oregano, thyme, chilli and bay leaves and mix well. — Pour the mixture over the chicken, moving it around so that the liquid and ingredients are evenly distributed. — Pour the olive oil over the top and season well. — Using a sieve, lightly dust the paprika over the top, then roast for 45–60 minutes, basting the chicken occasionally with the liquid, until the chicken is crisp-skinned and golden. — Allow to rest for at least 5 minutes before serving. — To serve, spoon into a serving dish with all the braising ingredients, top with fresh picked oregano and serve immediately, with green sauce forever to the side.

CHEF'S TIP
Chicken thighs are the best for this dish, skin on and bone in, both for their flavour and because they keep their shape.

Chicken fat rice

FROM THE PANTRY
Roasted chicken fat
(Basics, page 222)

Rice is always welcome at the table! This rice dish is based on a style of Persian crispy rice (*Tahdig*, pronounced tah-deeg, it literally means bottom of the pot), which is crisp on the top and soft and buttery on the inside. I have used the rendered chicken fat in this recipe, which you can also infuse with spices to give the dish more flavour. If you don't wish to use the chicken fat, you can replace it with butter or even olive oil.

TAHDIG-STYLE CHICKEN FAT RICE

500 g (1 lb 2 oz) jasmine rice

120 g (4½ oz) Greek yoghurt

120 g (4½ oz) Roasted chicken fat
(Basics, page 222)

Fill a 4 litre (135 fl oz) pot three-quarters full with water and bring to a rolling boil. — Season heavily with salt. — Put the rice in a large bowl and run cold water into the bowl until it is three-quarters full. — Using your hand, agitate the rice until the water is cloudy with starch. — Drain off the water, and refill with clean, cold water. — Repeat this process six times, or until the water runs clear. — Once the water is boiling, add the rice to the pot and bring the water back to the boil as quickly as possible. Once boiling, cook the rice for 6 minutes, stirring occasionally – it will still have an al dente bite to the grain. — Drain the rice through a sieve and run under cold water to stop it cooking. — Leave the rice to sit in the sieve over a bowl for a few minutes, until well drained. You should have just over 1 kg (2 lb 3 oz) of cooked rice. — Put 450 g (1 lb) of the rice in a separate bowl and mix with the yoghurt. — Heat a 28 cm (11 in) non-stick frying pan over a medium heat. — Add half the roasted chicken fat and melt it completely. — Add the rice and yoghurt mix and press the rice down all the way around the pan, to level it. — Add the remaining rice on top and spread it out evenly, pressing down and shaping it to the pan. — Now make 7 or 8 indentations in the rice by pressing down with the back of a wooden spoon – this will allow the moisture to escape and the rice to crisp. — Cook over a medium heat, making sure there is enough chicken fat in the pan to bubble around the sides of the rice; you can add more fat as the rice cooks by pouring it around the edges. — As a crust starts to form on the base of the pan and the rice turns a pale caramelised colour, turn the heat to low. You should soon be able to move the rice in the pan by gently rotating the entire 'cake' with your hands so it turns easily. Keep turning the rice cake a quarter turn each time, so that it cooks evenly. — Continue to cook the rice until caramelised, adding more chicken fat if required. — Once cooked, drain off any excess chicken fat, then flip the cake onto a warm serving plate with the crispy side facing up.

CHEF'S TIP

By all means, cook this beforehand, and reheat, uncovered, for 10 minutes at 150°C (300°F) before turning out to serve.

Use a quality non-stick pan with a heavy base for this dish.

Creamed sweetcorn, lime butter

PREP AHEAD
Make lime butter and refrigerate.

DAY BEFORE
Clean and trim corn.
Make corn custard.

ON THE DAY
Cook onions and corn.

In this dish, a childhood favourite grows up. This creamed sweetcorn is rich, velvety, sweet and salty, with a tangy lime butter that further accents its natural sweetness. We offered this dish at Sepia as part of a business lunch special, and people would always ask for the recipe so they could make it at home. Now they can.

LIME BUTTER

200 g (7 oz) unsalted butter, softened
zest of 1 lime
juice of ½ lime
1 teaspoon soy sauce
½ bunch (15 g/½ oz) tarragon, chopped
½ bunch (15 g/½ oz) chives, finely chopped

Put the butter into a bowl and beat with a spatula until light and fluffy. — Add the lime zest and juice, soy, tarragon and chives and continue to mix until completely combined. — Scrape the butter into an airtight container and refrigerate until required. — Allow to come to room temperature before serving.

CORN CUSTARD

3 corn cobs
50 g (1¾ oz) thickened (whipping) cream

Clean the corn from its husk and cut each cob in half to make it easy to handle. — Stand each half-cob on a board, cut-side down, then run the blade of a sharp knife down the corn to remove the kernels. Don't get too close to the core of the cob, as this will be too fibrous. — Set two-thirds of the kernels aside. — Blend the remaining one-third of the corn kernels using a liquidiser or hand-held blender until smooth, and pass through a fine strainer, making sure to squeeze as much out as possible. — Pour the corn liquid into a small, heavy-based saucepan. Add the cream, and cook gently over a low heat until the mixture coats the back of a spoon. Cool, then refrigerate in an airtight container until required.

CREAMED CORN

40 g (1½ oz) butter
1 brown onion, finely chopped
remaining corn kernels, as above
sea salt and freshly milled black pepper
Corn custard, as above
Lime butter, as above

Heat a saucepan over a medium heat, then add the butter. — Once the butter melts and starts to bubble, add the onion, sweating it until soft and transparent, without colouring. — Add the remaining corn kernels and gently sweat over a low–medium heat. — Season and cook for about 10 minutes, or until the corn is soft. — Add the corn custard and taste again for salt and pepper. — To serve, pour the creamed corn into a serving bowl and top with a good spoonful of soft lime butter.

CHEF'S TIP
The lime butter is a great accompaniment to other vegetables, too. Try adding it to steamed green beans or asparagus just before serving.

Broccolini, preserved lemon, macadamia

PREP AHEAD
Make preserved lemon dressing a few days prior.

DAY BEFORE
Roast macadamias and store.

Broccolini deserves an award for being the best all-rounder vegetable for family meals; good for steaming, boiling, roasting and perfect for barbecues and salads. This fabulous dressing will jazz it up a bit with the mellow tang of preserved lemon. Look for the smaller, slightly sweeter Moroccan style of preserved lemon, called *doqq* or *boussera*, which have a thinner skin and less pith.

PRESERVED LEMON DRESSING

100 g (3½ oz) preserved lemons, roughly chopped (I use baby preserved lemons from Morocco)

1 tablespoon preserved lemon brine, from the jar

zest and juice of 1 lemon

1½ tablespoons sugar

1 tablespoon lemon thyme leaves, lightly chopped

freshly milled black pepper

80 ml (2½ fl oz) olive oil

MAKES 200 G (7 OZ)

Combine all the ingredients except the olive oil in a blender and blitz until a puree is formed. — With the motor running on medium speed, drizzle in the oil in a slow steady stream, until emulsified. — Refrigerate in an airtight container.

MACADAMIAS

100 g (3½ oz) macadamia nuts

Heat the oven to 140°C (285°F). — Lay the macadamia nuts out on a tray and lightly spray with vegetable oil. Roast for 14–16 minutes, or until lightly golden in colour. — Give the tray a good shake halfway through the cooking to move the nuts around, ensuring they cook evenly. When done, remove from the oven and immediately transfer to a bowl to cool.

BROCCOLINI

3 broccolini stems

Remove the florets from the broccolini and refrigerate in an airtight container. — Cut the stems into small rounds and refrigerate in a separate airtight container.

TO SERVE

toasted macadamias, as above

1½ tablespoons olive oil

30 g (1 oz) butter

broccolini stems and florets, as above

80 g (2¾ oz) Preserved lemon dressing, as above

Coarsely chop three-quarters of the macadamias, and finely shave the remaining macadamias with a Microplane. Set aside in separate bowls. — Heat a sauté pan over a medium–high heat and add the olive oil and butter. — When the butter has melted and the mixture starts to bubble, add the sliced broccolini stems and sauté for about 1 minute. — Add the florets and continue to sauté until the broccolini turns bright green (adding a tablespoon of water will create steam and help them to cook). — Add the chopped macadamias and toss well. — Remove from the heat and pour over the preserved lemon dressing, tossing until well coated. — Season with pepper, spoon into a serving bowl, scatter with shaved macadamias and serve immediately.

CHEF'S TIP
The preserved lemon dressing is great with so many other vegetables, too, such as barbecued asparagus, as well as fish and meats such as grilled shoulder of lamb.

Lisbon chocolate cake

This is chocolate cake, but not as you know it. Rather than your classic baked sponge with chocolatey buttercream inside, it's a thing of textural utopia, a magical journey into chocolate bliss. Intense, but not too sweet nor too bitter, it's the perfect way to share the love with your family.

Known as Lisbon cake, or *bolo de chocolate cremoso*, it's the best reason to stop for a coffee in one of the famous cafes of Portugal. The secret is in the layers: a chocolate brownie base topped with ganache chocolate cream and a generous layer of rich, dark cocoa powder.

I've broken the recipe down into stages so you can make it in advance and relax on the day.

SPECIAL EQUIPMENT REQUIRED

22 cm (8¾ in) round cake tin with removable base

20 × 4 cm (8 × 1½ in) high cake ring

24 cm (9½ in) round cake board

22 × 6 cm (8¾ × 2½ in) high cake ring

6 cm (2½ in) high acetate

PREP AHEAD

Make the brownie a few days prior and freeze.

DAY BEFORE

Make all components and assemble cake.

ON THE DAY

Remove cake from the refrigerator 15 minutes prior.

BROWNIE

30 g (1 oz) butter, softened
150 g (5½ oz) dark chocolate (Valrhona Manjari 64%)
90 g (3 oz) butter
100 g (3½ oz) eggs, weighed without shells
60 g (2 oz) sugar
3 level tablespoons cake flour (or plain/all-purpose flour)
½ teaspoon baking powder

Heat the oven to 185°C (365°F). — Brush the base and sides of a 22 cm (8¾ in) cake tin with the soft butter. — Line the base with baking paper and brush again with the softened butter. — Break up the chocolate and put into a bowl, along with the 90 g (3 oz) butter. — Place the bowl over a pot of lightly simmering water, and slowly melt the chocolate and butter together, stirring. — Once melted, remove from the heat and set to one side. — Meanwhile, add the eggs to the bowl of a stand mixer. Using the whisk attachment, whip on high for 1 minute. — Add the sugar gradually while beating, and continue to beat until light and airy. — Stir the chocolate into the egg mixture. — Sift the flour and baking powder into a bowl and then fold the mixture through the egg and chocolate mixture to combine. — Pour the mixture into the cake tin, then use a finger palette knife to smooth over the surface. — Bake for 14–15 minutes, until the cake is still a little soft in the centre. Do not over bake, or it will be dry. — Remove from the oven and set on a wire rack to cool. — Once cooled, remove from the tin. Using a serrated knife, cut off the top to level the cake. — Using a 20 × 4 cm (8 × 1½ in) cake ring, cut out the centre of the cake, discarding the outside pieces. — Leave the cake in the ring and refrigerate in an airtight container.

GANACHE

100 g (3½ oz) thickened (whipping) cream
100 g (3½ oz) chocolate (Valrhona Manjari 64%)
30 g (1 oz) butter

Pour the cream into a small, heavy-based saucepan and bring to a simmer. — Break up the chocolate and put it in a heatproof jug. — Once the cream has boiled, pour it over the chocolate, and leave to sit for 30 seconds. — Using a hand-held blender, blitz the chocolate and cream until they emulsify and become smooth. — Add the butter and stir until silky and smooth. — Scrape down the sides of the jug and cover with plastic wrap. Set aside at room temperature until required.

CUSTARD

140 g (5 oz) thickened (whipping) cream
140 g (5 oz) full-cream milk
5 gelatine leaves, gold strength
60 g (2 oz) egg yolks
40 g (1½ oz) caster (superfine) sugar

MAKES 370 G (13 OZ)

Pour the cream and milk into a small saucepan and bring to a simmer. — Soak the gelatine in iced water for around 5 minutes to hydrate. — Meanwhile, whisk the egg yolks and sugar until pale and creamy. — When the cream and milk have boiled, pour them over the egg mixture, whisking constantly to combine. — Pour the mixture back into the saucepan and return to a low–medium heat. — Cook the egg mixture to 84°C (185°F), stirring continuously until the mixture thickens. Be careful not to overheat it, or the eggs will scramble and become lumpy. You should have a silky-smooth custard that coats the back of a spoon. — When that happens, remove from the heat. — Squeeze the excess water from the gelatine, then stir the gelatine through the still-hot custard until dissolved. — Pass the mixture through a fine sieve into a clean bowl, and set aside to cool to room temperature.

PREPARE THE CAKE

Brownie (page 121)

Ganache (page 121)

Spoon the ganache over the brownie in an even layer, then spread using a finger palette knife to make sure it is smooth and reaches right to the edges of the tin. — Refrigerate, to help set the ganache. Then, using a blowtorch, lightly warm the edges of the tin so that you can remove the cake easily. — Place the brownie with the ganache onto a 24 cm (9½ in) round cake board. — Spray the inside of a 22 × 6 cm (8¾ × 2½ in) high cake ring with olive-oil spray. — Cut enough 6 cm (2½ in) high acetate to go around the inside of the ring, with an extra 2 cm (¾ in) to overlap. — Spray the acetate with olive-oil spray, then put it inside the ring so the sprayed side of the acetate faces inwards. — Place this ring over the brownie and ganache, leaving a 1 cm (½ in) gap between the cake and the ring, then set aside.

CHOCOLATE MOUSSE

410 g (14½ oz) thickened (whipping) cream

270 g (9½ oz) Custard (page 121)

½ teaspoon salt

340 g (12 oz) milk chocolate (Valrhona Jivara 40%)

Pour the cream into the bowl of a stand mixer. — Using the whisk attachment, whip the cream to stiff peaks, then refrigerate until required. — Pour the custard and salt into a small saucepan and warm to around 65°C (150°F), stirring constantly. — Break up the chocolate and put it in a heatproof bowl. — Pour the custard over the chocolate and stir until the chocolate is melted. — Set aside and allow to cool to 35°C (95°F). — Fold the cream through the chocolate mixture in three batches, being careful not to knock out the air, and ensuring that the mixture is smooth and lump-free. — Pour the mousse into the prepared ring over and around the brownie and ganache, allowing it to get right down into the gap between the cake and the ring. — Once filled, hold the cake board and ring tightly with both hands and tap the board on the bench, to force the mousse into an even layer. — Smooth off the top and refrigerate for at least 4 hours.

TO SERVE

40 g (1½ oz) cocoa powder (Valrhona Dutch cocoa powder)

Once the mousse has set, remove the cake from the refrigerator, and remove the metal ring from the outside by sliding it upwards. — Remove the acetate by carefully peeling it away from the mousse. — Liberally dust the top of the cake with cocoa powder and clean up any excess chocolate. — Refrigerate until required. — Remove from the refrigerator 15 minutes prior to serving, to allow the mousse to warm and the chocolate flavour to open up.

SHARE THE LOVE

6 VARIETY IS THE SPICE OF LIFE

CANAPES / SNACKS
SERVED ON ARRIVAL

Prawn toasts, sansho and sesame

STARTERS
SERVED AS INDIVIDUAL DISHES

Tuna, chilli yoghurt, citrus soy jelly
Grilled miso toothfish, spicy citrus soy butter

MAINS & SIDES
SERVED TOGETHER ON THE TABLE

Blackened piri-piri chicken
Barbecued eggplants, 'nduja sesame
Heirloom tomatoes, toasted garlic oil, shichimi togarashi

DESSERT

Caramelised apple, miso butterscotch and almond semifreddo

WINE TIME

Blanc de Noirs Champagne
German Kabinett-style riesling
Dry chenin blanc
Light-bodied zweigelt (*best decanted before serving*)
Sweet butterscotch sauternes

COCKTAIL HOUR Manhattan 211

I grew up in regional England, in an era when food was changing rapidly from the bland, boiled and roasted, to take in influences being introduced via trading ports and immigration. As chefs reflected these changes in their dishes, our food suddenly got a whole lot more interesting. There wasn't just one way to do things anymore. You could tweak or tease a dish with a spice or spice paste and it would come alive as a completely different thing.

One single dish, chicken tikka masala, has become a symbol of that culinary multiculturalism, and is now widely considered Britain's national dish – a long way from the roast beef and potatoes of yore.

As I travelled and cooked all over the world, I discovered more and more spices, peppers and chillies to incorporate into my cooking, many of which are listed in the Basics section in this book.

This menu is my homage to the difference that spices make to your cooking. Every dish is built around a spice, pepper or chilli, but it's used in a way that complements rather than overpowers. In the same way, the menu doesn't follow one set cuisine, but uses the freedom we have in Australia to express ourselves with what we have to hand and what we have learnt. There's a wide, wonderful, open world of spices out there that is free of borders; as you'll discover when you add the Japanese sansho pepper in the Cantonese prawn toast appetiser, or experience the wonderful effect of shichimi togarashi sprinkles on a simple salad of sliced tomatoes. That's the sort of tiny revelation that chefs love – and that guests love, too.

Balance is, of course, key; more so with spices than anything. Just because you're using spices doesn't mean you shouldn't season your food; it still needs salt. And if you feel something could do with more spice, do it!

And remember, not all chilli needs to blow your head off. Some fragrant chillies add a subtle complexity that's so much more than just heat. I often harness the power of hot chilli with a cooling component such as yoghurt, as in the entrée of yellow fin tuna with chilli yoghurt and citrus soy jelly. Smoked paprika is the secret of everyone's favourite piri-piri chicken, and I've included a good tip in the recipe to make sure it infuses right through the chicken.

The only dish in this menu that is spice-free is the spectacular dessert of creamy caramelised apple and miso butterscotch semifreddo. Here, I've borrowed a trick from numerous spice-loving cultures by finishing with something dairy based, for its refreshing, tempering qualities. There's nothing better than a cooling ice cream as the final flourish of a great get-together.

THE PLAYLIST **BONOBO** Migration **DAVID BOWIE** Hunky Dory **EVERYTHING BUT TH FLEETWOOD MAC** Rumours **FKA TWIGS** LP1 **KENDRICK LAMAR** To Pimp a Butter **THE VELVET UNDERGROUND** Velvet Underground and Nico

IRL Walking Wounded **FLUKE** Progressive History XXX **MORCHEEBA** Big Calm
GY POP Préliminaires **MASSIVE ATTACK** Collected **SNOH AALEGRA** Feels

Prawn toasts, sansho and sesame

FROM THE PANTRY
Shellfish oil (Basics, page 225)

DAY BEFORE
Make prawn mix and refrigerate.

ON THE DAY
Assemble toasts and refrigerate.
You can fry 1 hour prior and
keep warm.

With fond memories from my time living in Hong Kong, I bequeath to you this fun twist on the dim sum classic that everyone loves. Prawn (shrimp) toast is the perfect appetizer because it goes so well with Champagne or a cocktail, and it's satisfying without being too rich.

PRAWN MIX

500 g (1 lb 2 oz) (about 6) whole king prawns (shrimp), U6 size
1 teaspoon sansho pepper or Sichuan pepper, ground
1 tablespoon Shellfish oil (Basics, page 225)
1 teaspoon salt

TOASTS

3 × mini milk buns, or brioche-style mini burger buns
Prawn mix, as above
40 g (1½ oz) white sesame seeds (not toasted)

TO SERVE

1.5 litres (51 fl oz) vegetable oil
salt and sansho pepper, for sprinkling

MAKES 210 G (7½ OZ)

Peel the prawns (freeze the shells for future shellfish oils or stocks). — Remove the intestinal tract from the prawns and discard. — Arrange the prawns on a tray lined with paper towel and cover with more paper towel. Leave for 1 hour to absorb excess moisture. — Chop the prawns into a coarse paste, and season with sansho pepper, shellfish oil and salt. — Mix well together to make a sticky paste, then refrigerate in an airtight container.

Cut the milk buns in half. Divide the prawn mix evenly over the 6 halves, then use a palette knife or spatula to spread it evenly over each cut side. — Pour the sesame seeds into a bowl and dip the prawn coating into the sesame seeds. — Place on a tray and refrigerate until required.

Heat the oven to 50°C (120°F). — Line a tray with paper towel and set to one side. — Heat the oil in a large, heavy-based pot until the temperature reaches 195°C (385°F). — Turn the heat to low. — Working with two at a time, gently put the prawn breads in the oil, prawn-side up, and fry for around 1 minute. Flip over and fry for a further minute, or until the sesame seeds are golden. — Lift out with a wire strainer or slotted spoon and place prawn-side down on the lined tray to remove excess oil, then flip over and season with salt and sansho pepper. — Keep warm in the oven while you fry the remaining prawn buns. — Place on a serving plate and serve immediately.

CHEF'S TIP
You can use different species of prawns, such as banana, tiger or king, and indeed, different sizes. Bear in mind that once peeled and cleaned, the prawn meat will be roughly 40 per cent of the total weight.

I prefer to buy green (raw) prawns frozen, and defrost as needed, to control freshness and reduce waste. Most prawns in the shops have been frozen and thawed anyway.

Tuna, chilli yoghurt, citrus soy jelly

Ponzu sauce
(Basics, page 222)

My fermented chilli
(Basics, page 221)

Crispy rayu chilli
(Basics, page 215)

Fragrant chilli oil
(Basics, page 216)

DAY BEFORE

Make citrus soy jelly.

Hang yoghurt and refrigerate.

Prepare tuna and refrigerate.

ON THE DAY

Dice jellies and refrigerate.

Dice tuna and refrigerate.

Marinate tuna just prior to
serving.

Up your tartare game with this spicy tuna teamed with chilli-inflected sheep's milk yoghurt.

This makes an incredibly refreshing entrée, especially when topped with zingy, chewy, citrus soy sauce jelly, as it is here. Dig out some fancy glassware and bring a sparkle to your table.

CITRUS SOY JELLY

7 gelatine leaves, gold strength	
115 ml (4 fl oz) water	
360 ml (12 fl oz) Ponzu sauce (Basics, page 222)	

Prepare a 750–1000 ml (25½–34 fl oz) container by lightly spraying with oil then wiping with paper towel, so that a fine layer of the oil remains. — Soak the gelatine in iced water for about 5 minutes, until soft and pliable. — Squeeze out as much water as possible and set aside in a bowl. — Bring the water to a boil in a saucepan, then remove from the heat. — Add the gelatine and stir until dissolved, then pour in the ponzu sauce, stirring to combine. — Strain into the prepared container and allow to cool, then set in the fridge for at least 6 hours. — Once set, turn out the jelly onto a board. — Cut the jelly into 1 cm (½ in) wide slices. Lay them out flat and cut each slice into 1 cm (½ in) thick strips, then cut each strip into 1 cm (½ in) dice. (Tip: it's easier to turn the board than it is to move the jellies.) — Use a pastry scraper to scoop the jelly into an airtight container and refrigerate until required.

SHEEP'S YOGHURT AND CHILLI

500 g (1 lb 2 oz) sheep's milk yoghurt	
2 tablespoons My Fermented chilli (Basics, page 221) or store bought	

MAKES 350 G (12½ OZ)

Pour the yoghurt into a sieve set above a bowl, and leave in the refrigerator to strain for around 5 hours. — Discard the whey, or use in a dressing. — Pass the strained yoghurt through a fine sieve then add the fermented chilli paste, stirring to combine. — Refrigerate in an airtight container until required.

TUNA

500 g (1 lb 2 oz) sashimi-grade tuna loin	
2 tablespoons olive oil	
2 good pinches ground white pepper	
1½ tablespoons soy sauce	
1 tablespoon mirin	
2 tablespoons finely snipped chives	
2 tablespoons Crispy rayu chilli (Basics, page 215)	
2 teaspoons Fragrant chilli oil (Basics, page 216), optional	

Trim the tuna, making sure it's clean of scales and any bloodline. Wrap in paper towel, then in plastic wrap, and refrigerate for a good 6 hours prior to using. — Place the rested tuna on a cutting board, remove the wrapping, and cut into slices 1 cm (½ in) thick. Arrange the slices neatly on the board. — Cut each slice into 1 cm (½ in) thick strips, then turn and cut each strip into 1 cm (½ in) dice. — Use a pastry scraper to scoop the diced tuna into an airtight container and refrigerate until required. — To marinate the tuna just before serving, run a spoon through it to help separate the cubes, then drizzle with the olive oil, stirring gently to coat. — Season with white pepper, soy and mirin, turning over gently until evenly coated. — Fold in the chives, crispy rayu chilli, and fragrant chilli oil if using. — Cover and refrigerate until required.

TO SERVE

Sheep's yoghurt and chilli, as above	
Tuna, as above	
Citrus soy jelly, as above	
olive oil, to drizzle	

Place two spoonfuls of sheep's yoghurt and chilli on the base of each individual bowl. — Divide the tuna between the bowls, spooning it over the yoghurt to cover. — Spoon the jelly into a bowl and lightly drizzle with olive oil, then spoon the jelly over the tuna and serve immediately.

CHEF'S TIP
Find a fishmonger you trust, and place an order for the fish in advance, specifying sashimi-grade. If you don't want to use tuna, try salmon, bonito or albacore.

Grilled miso toothfish, spicy citrus soy butter

FROM THE PANTRY
Miso marinade
(Basics, page 220)

Ponzu sauce
(Basics, page 222)

Korean-style chilli paste
(Basics, page 218)

PREP AHEAD
Marinate fish 4 days prior.

ON THE DAY
Remove fish from marinade.
Make sauce.

A close relative to the Antarctic toothfish, Glacier 51 toothfish is also known as Patagonian toothfish or Chilean sea bass, named for the 51st glacier off Heard Island in Australian waters, some 2000 kilometres (1200 miles) off the Western Australian coast. It's processed and filleted at sea, and snap-frozen for a premium, luxury market here and in Japan. It's a revelation; the high fat and omega-3 content and large, scalloping flakes give amazing mouthfeel and flavour.

A traditional miso marinade is a perfect match, lightly curing the fish while also imparting flavour, and the citrus soy butter elevates it to dinner party status.

TO MARINATE THE TOOTHFISH

6 × 120–140 g (4½–5 oz) portions Glacier 51 toothfish, or any other thick white-fleshed fatty fish

600 g (1 lb 5 oz) Miso marinade (Basics, page 220)

Make sure the fish is clean of any scales. — Place fish on a tray lined with paper towel, and cover with more paper towel. Refrigerate for at least 2–3 hours, to help remove excess moisture. — Pour the miso marinade into a container wide enough to fit the toothfish portions side by side. — Submerge the toothfish in the marinade then cover with plastic wrap, pressing it down onto the fish. Put a lid on the container and refrigerate for 3–4 days, turning the fish after the first 2 days and making sure it is well coated. — Remove the fish from the container and wipe off any excess marinade, then refrigerate on a tray, uncovered, for up to 6 hours prior to cooking.

SPICY CITRUS SOY BUTTER

250 g (9 oz) butter

180 g (6½ oz) Ponzu sauce (Basics, page 222)

2 teaspoons Korean-style chilli paste (Basics, page 218) or gochujang

Heat a small, heavy-based saucepan over a medium heat, then add the butter. — Cook until the butter starts to bubble and caramelise. — Once the butter is nut brown and smells toasty, whisk in the ponzu sauce. — Bring to a simmer while whisking, then remove from the heat. — Add the Korean-style chilli paste then blitz the sauce using a hand-held blender until emulsified. — Leave at room temperature until required.

TO SERVE

marinated fish, as above

2 teaspoons Korean-style chilli paste (Basics, page 218) or gochujang

salt

Spicy citrus soy butter, as above

Heat the oven to 240°C (465°F). — Put a heavy cast-iron roasting tray or pan into the oven and heat for 10 minutes. — Meanwhile, lightly brush the fish with the chilli paste and season with salt — When hot, carefully remove the pan from the oven, add a little oil to the pan, then place the toothfish on top. — Bake for around 6–7 minutes, until golden and cooked. — Keep warm, while you heat the spicy citrus soy butter and blitz again to emulsify. — Pour the citrus soy butter onto a high-rimmed serving platter, arrange the fish on top and serve immediately.

CHEF'S TIP
Alternatively, cook the fish over a barbecue until golden and caramelised. I suggest you skewer the fish first, so you can regulate its height, rather than place it directly on the grill bars, as the marinade might burn when it comes into close contact with the flame.

Blackened piri-piri chicken

Best-ever brine
(Basics, page 214)

Korean-style chilli paste
(Basics, page 218)

PREP AHEAD

Make the brine.

DAY BEFORE

Spatchcock or butterfly
the chicken.

Brine the chicken.

ON THE DAY

Roast the chicken prior
to guests arriving.

Make the sauce.

If you haven't brined chicken before, you are in for an epiphany. Brining makes the flesh so juicy and full of flavour – just make sure you have room in the refrigerator first! This is adapted from the famously spicy, charcoal-grilled piri-piri chicken of Portugal, one of the world's great chicken dishes. Coated with paprika and chilli paste, the skin is dramatically blackened, but the chicken doesn't dry out. Served with a sauce made from the lemony roasting juices, this is a great dish to share with friends.

TO PREPARE THE CHICKEN

1.8 kg (4 lb) whole
free-range chicken

1 batch of Best-ever brine
(Basics, page 214)

1 tablespoon smoked hot paprika

100 g (3½ oz) Korean-style chilli
paste (Basics, page 218),
or gochujang

Rinse the chicken under cold water, then pat dry with paper towel. — Using a paring knife, remove the wishbone by scraping along the side of the bone on each side. — Use your fingers to find the top of the bone, then pinch and twist to pull it out. — Place the chicken on a cutting board breast-side down, cavity hole facing you. — Using heavy-duty scissors or poultry shears, cut either side of the backbone all the way through to the tail. — Once cut through on both sides, remove the backbone and discard. — Turn the chicken over and, using both hands, press down gently but firmly to flatten. — Add the brine to a large enough container to hold both brine and chicken. — Submerge the chicken completely in the brine, cover with a lid and refrigerate for 12–16 hours. — Drain well, discarding the brine, then pat the chicken dry with paper towel. — Place the chicken on a wire rack set on a tray. — Using a small sieve, dust the skin of the chicken with paprika. — Refrigerate for an hour to let the paprika dry onto the skin. — Brush the chicken all over, including the underside, with the chilli paste, then refrigerate for 3–4 hours.

TO COOK THE CHICKEN

2 lemons, cut into quarters

sea salt and pepper

40 ml (1¼ fl oz) olive oil

prepared chicken, as above

Put the lemon quarters into a bowl and season well with salt and pepper. — Add the olive oil, tossing to coat. — Put the lemon wedges in a heavy roasting dish, spread out to cover the centre of the dish, then add 200 ml (7 fl oz) water. — Place the chicken on top of the lemons, breast-side up. — Leave to sit at room temperature for 45 minutes before roasting. — Heat the oven to 220°C (430°F). When hot, roast the chicken for 45 minutes, turning the dish around halfway through to ensure an even colouring of the skin. — Allow the chicken to rest for at least 40 minutes in a warm place. — Strain the pan juices and lemons through a sieve into a clean small pan and set aside.

TO SERVE

100 ml (3½ fl oz) chicken and the
lemon roasting juices, as above

1 tablespoon extra-virgin olive oil

1 tablespoon red-wine vinegar, e.g.
Forvm cabernet sauvignon

Warm the roasting juices in a small saucepan, and whisk in the olive oil and vinegar until emulsified. — Season if required and keep warm. — Serve the chicken either whole, or cut into pieces. — To joint the chicken, first remove the wing tips and the wings. — Remove both legs, then cut each leg in half at the thigh bone joint, giving you two drumsticks and two thighs. — Place the wings, drumsticks and thighs on a warm serving dish. — Remove both breasts by cutting down the breastbone. — Cut each breast into 6 even slices and place on the serving dish. — Pour over the lemon sauce and serve immediately. — Alternatively, pour the sauce onto the base of a serving plate, place the whole chicken on top, and carve at the table.

CHEF'S TIP

Ask your butcher to butterfly
the chicken if you are not
comfortable doing this yourself.

Discard the brine after use,
as it contains live bacteria.

Barbecued eggplants, 'nduja sesame

Seasoned rice-wine vinegar
(Basics, page 224)

Chicken stock (Basics, page 215)

Sweet smoked paprika oil
(Basics, page 226)

DAY BEFORE

Make the sesame seed salt.

Barbecue eggplants (aubergines),
drain and store.

ON THE DAY

Make 'nduja and sesame sauce.

Eggplant (aubergine) is another of those vegetables that absorbs big, bold flavours like a sponge – and 'nduja, that soft, spreadable, chilli-hot Calabrian salami, is a big, bold flavour. Use the barbecue to really char and blacken the outside of the skin. This will not only make the skin easier to remove but will also give the flesh a beautiful smoky flavour. A great side dish, this is nutty, buttery, smoky and spicy all in one.

SESAME SEED SALT

20 g (¾ oz) white sesame seed

½ teaspoon sea salt flakes

Toast the sesame seeds in a frying pan over a low–medium heat for 3–4 minutes, swirling the pan so that the oils in the seeds don't scorch or burn. — When toasty and fragrant, remove from the heat, pour onto a tray and allow to cool. — Crush the salt flakes and sesame seeds in a mortar and pestle until they resemble coarse crumbs, then store in an airtight container.

EGGPLANT

4 × 250 g (9 oz) firm
eggplants (aubergines)

Turn the barbecue to high and close the lid, letting the internal temperature reach 300°C (570°F). — Lightly prick the eggplants with a small skewer, so that they do not explode while cooking. — When the barbecue is hot, chargrill the eggplants on all sides., making sure each part is blackened before you turn it. — The eggplants will start to deflate and collapse on themselves. — At this point, remove, put them in a bowl, cover with plastic wrap, and leave to cool completely. — Once cool, remove all the charred skin and discard. — Cut each eggplant in half lengthways and remove any excess seeds from the centre. — Line a tray with a few layers of paper towel, then lay the eggplants cut-side down on the tray to drain for as long as possible – overnight, for best results. — Cover and refrigerate for a few hours.

'NDUJA AND SESAME SAUCE

100 ml (3½ fl oz) Seasoned rice-wine vinegar (Basics, page 224)

2 shallots (60 g/2 oz in total), peeled and thinly sliced

200 ml (7 fl oz) Chicken stock (Basics, page 215)

100 g (3½ oz) butter, diced and chilled

25 g (1 oz) 'nduja salami

35 g (1¼ oz) sesame paste (tahini or goma)

In a heavy-based saucepan, add the seasoned rice-wine vinegar and shallots. — Bring to a simmer and reduce until almost all the vinegar has evaporated. — Add the chicken stock and reduce again, until the liquid is half the original volume. — Turn the heat to low, then slowly whisk in the butter, a few cubes at a time, until incorporated. — Continue whisking constantly, and do not let the sauce boil. — Once the butter is incorporated, remove from the heat and strain the sauce through a fine sieve into a clean small saucepan. — Break the 'nduja into small pieces and add it to the butter sauce along with the sesame paste. — Using a hand-held blender, blitz the sauce until smooth and emulsified, then set aside.

TO SERVE

Barbecued eggplants, as above

'Nduja and sesame sauce, as above

2 tablespoons Sweet smoked paprika oil (Basics, page 226)

Sesame seed salt, as above

Heat the oven to 160°C (320°F). — Put the eggplants in a heatproof dish and warm in the oven for 6–7 minutes, to heat through. — Meanwhile, return the 'nduja and sesame sauce to the stove and warm to around 65°C (150°F), whisking constantly. — Arrange the warm eggplant on a high-rimmed serving plate. — Blitz the sauce again using a hand-held blender, then add half the paprika oil. — Spoon the butter sauce over the eggplants and drizzle with remaining paprika oil. — Scatter with the sesame seed salt, and serve immediately.

CHEF'S TIP

If you find 'nduja too spicy, keep an eye out for sobrasada, a gently spiced, paprika-tainted cured pork sausage from the Balearic Islands.

Heirloom tomatoes, toasted garlic oil, shichimi togarashi

Toasted garlic oil
(Basics, page 227)

ON THE DAY
Slice tomatoes just prior
to guest arrival.

Salt and oil tomatoes
15 minutes prior to serving.

Sometimes, you just have to let the produce do the talking. This simple dish is all about letting heirloom tomatoes be true to themselves, drizzled with toasted garlic oil and spiced with a little Japanese shichimi togarashi. Look for a few different varieties and colours of tomatoes; the end result will be like a dazzling patchwork quilt.

Always serve tomatoes at room temperature, never chilled, and season with sea salt 15 minutes before serving, to draw out the flavour.

PREPARE AND SERVE THE TOMATOES

400 g (14 oz) heirloom tomatoes
a few good pinches of sea salt
2 tablespoons Toasted garlic oil (Basics, page 227)
a few good shakes of shichimi togarashi pepper, store bought

Thinly slice the tomatoes and arrange on a serving plate with an eye for colour. — Season with salt and drizzle with toasted garlic oil. — Leave to sit at room temperature for 15 minutes before serving. — Sprinkle with shichimi pepper, and serve immediately.

CHEF'S TIP
Always purchase your tomatoes a week prior to using, and leave them at room temperature, so they ripen and become sweet. Never put them in the refrigerator, which deadens the flavour.

Caramelised apple, miso butterscotch and almond semifreddo

Make toasted almonds, miso butterscotch and caramelised apple.

DAY BEFORE

Make mascarpone cream, Italian meringue and pâte à bombe.

Assemble semifreddo and freeze.

ON THE DAY

AM

Unmould semifreddo and return to freezer.

Go big, or go home! I have deliberately super-sized this magnificent semifreddo (also known as an icebox cake) in a large, high tin measuring 22 × 22 × 7 cm (8¾ × 8¾ × 2¾ in), because it looks so impressive; the perfect celebration ice-cream cake.

You could do it in two loaf tins measuring 22 × 12 × 7 cm (8¾ × 4¾ × 2¾ in) instead, or halve the recipe – although I find that stand mixers give much better aeration when the volume is high, rather than low.

There's a bit to do, but I've broken it down into components that you can prepare two days in advance, to give you plenty of wiggle room on the day.

TOASTED ALMONDS

250 g (9 oz) flaked almonds

Heat the oven to 160°C (320°F). — Arrange almonds in a single layer on a large baking tray (or two smaller ones) and bake for 14–16 minutes, turning the tray and tossing the almonds every 5 or 6 minutes. — Once golden, transfer to a cool tray or marble bench to quickly cool. — Once cool, store in an airtight container.

MISO BUTTERSCOTCH

200 g (7 oz) thickened (whipping) cream

120 g (4½ oz) unsalted butter

120 g (4½ oz) Saikyo miso or shiro miso

160 g (5½ oz) light muscovado sugar

60 g (2 oz) liquid glucose

Heat the cream and butter together in a heavy-based pot until the butter has melted. — Whisk in the miso, sugar and glucose. — Turn the heat to medium–high and bring the mixture to a boil, then simmer until thick and caramelised. — Blitz the mixture with a hand-held blender until smooth, then pass through a fine sieve into a container. — Allow to cool at room temperature.

CARAMELISED APPLE

250 g (9 oz) caster (superfine) sugar

4 granny smith apples, or other tart cooking apples, peeled, cored and quartered

1 teaspoon vanilla paste

1 teaspoon sea salt

50 ml (1¾ fl oz) Calvados

To make a dry caramel, start by heating a wide-bottomed saucepan over a medium heat. — Add one-third of the sugar to cover the base of the pan, and allow it to slowly melt. — As the sugar melts, it will turn golden in colour and become fluid – be careful not to heat it too quickly, or the sugar will burn. — Once melted, add another third of the sugar and repeat the process until the sugar has melted into the caramel. — Add the last third of the sugar and repeat the process until all the sugar has melted. — Once the caramel is dark golden, carefully add the apple quarters and cook for 7–8 minutes, until plump and soft, gently stirring the caramel to help them cook evenly. — In a bowl, mix together the vanilla, salt and Calvados and then add this mixture to the caramel. Be careful, as the caramel will produce steam and bubble up. — Cook until the apples become almost translucent, then set aside and allow the apples to cool and absorb the syrup.

WHIPPED MASCARPONE CREAM

165 g (6 oz) mascarpone cheese

300 g (10½ oz) thickened (whipping) cream

MAKES 460 G (1 LB)

To a bowl, add the mascarpone cheese and 100 g (3½ oz) of the cream and mix until smooth. — Pour the remaining cream into the bowl of a stand mixer and, using the whisk attachment, whip the cream to soft peaks. — Add the mascarpone and cream mixture and whip until you have medium–stiff peaks. — Refrigerate until required.

ITALIAN MERINGUE

120 g (4½ oz) egg whites

pinch of cream of tartar

180 g (6½ oz) sugar

MAKES 250 G (9 OZ)

Add the egg whites and cream of tartar to the bowl of a stand mixer. — Using the whisk attachment, slowly whip the mixture at low–medium speed. — Meanwhile, add the sugar and 70 ml (2¼ fl oz) water to a small, heavy-based saucepan and heat to 121°C (250°F), using a thermometer. — When the temperature is around 114°C (235°F), turn the speed up on the stand mixer and whip the egg whites to soft peaks. — Once the temperature reaches 121°C (250°F), remove the syrup from the heat and, while still whisking, slowly pour it into the egg whites. — Continue to whip until the meringue cools, then remove from the mixer and set aside.

PÂTE À BOMBE

220 g (8 oz) sugar

220 g (8 oz) egg yolks

1 teaspoon vanilla paste

MAKES 400 G (14 OZ)

Pour the sugar and 70 ml (2¼ fl oz) water into a small, clean, heavy-based saucepan and place over a medium heat. — Meanwhile, combine the egg yolks and vanilla in the bowl of a stand mixer. Using the whisk attachment, whip the yolks on high speed until they double in size and become light and airy. — Bring the sugar and water to 121°C (250°F). At this stage, remove the syrup from the heat and pour it slowly into the egg yolks, while still whipping. — Continue to whip until the eggs are cooled, then set aside.

TO ASSEMBLE THE SEMIFREDDO

400 g (14 oz) Pâte à bombe, as above

440 g (15½ oz) Whipped mascarpone cream, (page 141)

200 g (7 oz) Italian meringue, as above

500 g (1 lb 2 oz) Caramelised apple (page 141), drained (reserve the caramel; see Chef's tip below)

200 g (7 oz) amaretti biscuits (store bought), crumbled

120 g (4½ oz) Miso butterscotch (page 141), reserve the remainder for serving

ONCE YOU HAVE PREPARED ALL THE COMPONENTS, WEIGH THEM TO GET THE AMOUNTS FOR THIS SECTION.

Spray a 22 × 22 × 7 cm (8¾ × 8¾ × 2¾) square cake tin with a removable base with baker's spray and line the base with baking paper. — Alternatively, use two 22 × 12 × 7 cm (8¾ × 4¾ × 2¾ in) loaf tins. — Prepare another sheet of baking paper in advance, for the top of the semifreddo. — Put the pâte à bombe in an extra-large bowl, and fold in the mascarpone cream. — Once smooth, fold in the Italian meringue until smooth and airy. — Break the caramelised apple into chunks and fold through the mixture. — Fold in the crumbled amaretti biscuits, being careful not to lose too much air. — Drizzle in the miso butterscotch and lightly fold through to give a rippled effect. — Pour the mixture into the prepared tin and tap down to make even, then top with the baking paper, pressing down lightly until flat and even. — Wrap the tin in plastic wrap to completely seal the semifreddo on all sides, then freeze for 6 hours. — After 6 hours, remove the semifreddo and wrap it in a tea towel (dish towel), to stop ice crystals from forming, then return to the freezer. — Freeze for at least another 12 hours before serving.

TO SERVE THE SEMIFREDDO

250 g (9 oz) toasted flaked almonds

160 g (5½ oz) Miso butterscotch (page 141)

Remove the semifreddo from the freezer and unwrap. — Place a 24 cm (9½ in) square cake board on top of the tin, then flip the semifreddo onto the cake board. — Use your hands to warm the sides and base of the tin for a few minutes. — To unmould, press down gently on the base of the tin, but do not force it. — The semifreddo should eventually slide out onto the cake board. — Return to the freezer until you are ready to serve. — Put the almonds in a heatproof bowl. — Warm the miso butterscotch in a small saucepan over a medium heat, or in the microwave, until warm and fluid. — Pour the butterscotch over the almonds, tossing well until they all stick together. — Remove the semifreddo from the freezer and arrange the almonds on top. — Serve immediately, with any remaining miso butterscotch on the side.

CHEF'S TIP

Where Italian meringue is made by pouring sugar cooked to 121°C (250°F) into whipping egg whites, pâte à bombe is made by pouring the sugar syrup into whipping egg yolks instead. This technique is used in commercial cakes and desserts to pasteurise the egg yolks.

Reserve the caramel strained from the apples and use for pouring over ice cream to add that extra special topping.

7 UP THE GARDEN PATH

CANAPES / SNACKS
SERVED ON ARRIVAL

Radishes, lemon yoghurt, black sesame salt
Comté, olives, pickled onions
Potato tart with red leicester, coriander seeds

STARTERS
SERVED AS INDIVIDUAL DISHES

White bean peanut butter hummus, Greek salad
Peas, please!

MAINS & SIDES
SERVED TOGETHER ON THE TABLE

Eggplant rotolo
Butternut, burrata, roasted chilli

DESSERT

Coconut rice, maraschino cherries, shaved chocolate

WINE TIME

Non-vintage sparkling wine
Aromatic Sancerre
Savoury Rhône Valley white blend
Medium-bodied cabernet franc
Sweet fortified white wine

COCKTAIL HOUR The Last Word 211

This menu is purely vegetarian – but it is not purely for vegetarians. Instead, it's a beautiful dinner party that everyone at the table can enjoy.

After all, who doesn't love an oozy, cheesy potato tart, or a creamy white bean hummus served with a crunchy dice of all the elements of a Greek salad?

Crack open the red wine for a deeply flavoured pasta rotolo stuffed with eggplant (aubergine) and red peppers (bell peppers), and a racy little side of chilli-slathered butternut pumpkin (squash) with burrata nestling in its hollows.

After years of owning and running a restaurant, I have seen every type of food preference and dietary requirement – sometimes, all in the one service! – and I have tried very hard to honour them all. This has taught me how to pivot quickly to new ingredients, and how to build flavour into dishes that are meat-free, because I want everyone to have the same good time. After all, everyone comes to a restaurant with the same high expectations, no matter what they can or can't eat – and so they should.

It's a similar scenario with a dinner party. You want everyone to have the same good time, and not be the poor person at the end of the table saying 'no, don't worry, I'll just have the salad'.

So here are a few of the things I've learnt. A menu free of meat and fish isn't just about vegetables – you still need to build in protein in the form of lentils, beans or chickpeas. Explore the wonderful world of seaweed, miso pastes and ferments for their deep umami flavours. Use the barbecue to give your veg, a wonderful smoky char – something that works especially well with sweetcorn, eggplant, peppers, onions and the more robust leafy greens.

Build up a pantry of pickles, mustards and citrussy relishes that add pops of flavour and intrigue. Intensify mouthfeel and textural contrast with crushed nuts, crispy fried onions and grilled flat breads. Stay as seasonal as you can to get the utmost flavour out of springtime peas or autumnal mushrooms. And, above all, make a spectacular dessert!

This is one garden path we can all be led up, quite happily.

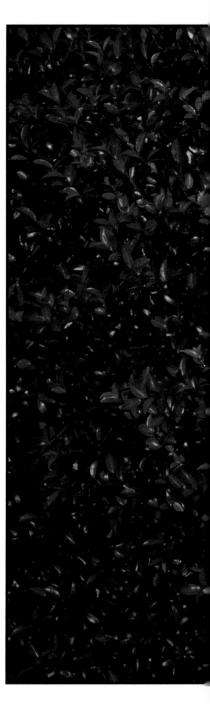

THE PLAYLIST **BLUE STATES** Nothing Changes Under the Sun **BOY & BEAR** Harlequ **L'IMPÉRATRICE** Tako Tsubo **MANSIONAIR** Shadowboxer **MONSTER RAL SAINT ETIENNE** Foxbase Alpha **SON LITTLE** Son Little **DJ KRUSH** Butterfly Effec

146   **THE DINNER PARTY**

ream **COCTEAU TWINS** Stars and Topsoil **DEEP DIVE CORP.** Freestyle Floating
otanica Dream **NOT DROWNING. WAVING** Another Pond **RADIOHEAD** OK Computer

Radishes, lemon yoghurt, black sesame salt

FROM THE PANTRY
Lemon olive oil
(Basics, page 218)

One of the finest ways to begin a meal in France is to dip a fresh, crunchy little radish into butter and eat it with sea salt. This is my little twist on the classic, using the drama of black sesame salt and creamy goat's yoghurt for a zing of acidity.

PREP AHEAD
Make black sesame salt.
Drain goat's yoghurt.

DAY BEFORE
Prepare goat's yoghurt and store.
Wash radishes and store.

BLACK SESAME SALT

3 level tablespoons black sesame seeds	
1 teaspoon sea salt flakes	

Pour the sesame seeds into a frying pan. — Place the pan over a low–medium heat and gently toast, swirling the pan so that the oils in the sesame seeds do not scorch or burn. — Toast for 3–4 minutes, until toasty and fragrant, then remove from the heat and pour onto a tray. Allow to cool. — Put the salt flakes and sesame seeds into a mortar and pestle, and crush together until you have a coarse crumb. — Store in an airtight container.

GOAT'S YOGHURT

500 g (1 lb 2 oz) goat's yoghurt	
zest of 1 lemon	
freshly milled black pepper	

MAKES 350 G (12½ OZ)

Pour the yoghurt into a fine sieve set over a bowl and refrigerate for around 5 hours, to strain out the liquid whey. You should get about 150 g (5½ oz) whey in the bowl. (This can be reserved and used for dressings and vinaigrettes.) — Once strained, pass the yoghurt through a fine sieve, then add the lemon zest and black pepper, stirring until combined. — Refrigerate in an airtight container until required.

RADISHES

250 g (9 oz), (around 15) baby belle radishes	

Wash the radishes and trim the stems, leaving a centimetre or 2 of the green stems, and pat dry with a paper towel. — Keep refrigerated in ice-cold water until required.

TO SERVE

200 g (7 oz) Goat's yoghurt, as above	
Radishes, as above	
20 ml (¾ fl oz) Lemon olive oil (Basics, page 218)	
1 tablespoon Black sesame salt, as above	

Spoon the yoghurt into the centre of a serving plate. — Cut each radish in half from stem to root and place around the yoghurt in a spiral design, cut-side up. — Drizzle with lemon olive oil, scatter with black sesame salt and serve.

CHEF'S TIP
Any leftover black sesame salt is ideal for seasoning mixed leaf salads, or over vegetable dishes such as grilled or roasted cauliflower. It's also brilliant with a bowl of rice.

Keeping the radishes whole in iced water will keep them fresh, vibrant and crunchy.

Comté, olives, pickled onions

DAY BEFORE
Stuff olives and marinate.
Cut Comté into cubes and store.

ON THE DAY
Make up skewers and store.

It's skewer time! Everyone loves eating food from a stick, and these skewers are a far more sophisticated version of that 1970s dinner party favourite of cheese and pineapple. This is all about elevating the idea with quality ingredients and serving them on beautiful decorative cocktail skewers for another level of charm.

Comté is one of the great cheeses of the world. Sicilian olives stuffed with roasted piquillo peppers are bright and fruity, and little bright-red pearl onions give everything a retro-cool lift.

STUFFED OLIVES

12 Sicilian green olives
(e.g. Castelvetrano), pitted

30 g (1 oz) Navarrico roasted
piquillo peppers

extra-virgin olive oil, to cover

Drain the olives and set to one side. — Drain the piquillo peppers, pat dry and cut into thin strips. — With the help of a skewer, push a strip of piquillo pepper into each olive. — Put in an airtight container and cover with olive oil. If making in advance, refrigerate until required, otherwise store at room temperature.

TO SERVE

130 g (4½ oz) Comté cheese

12 stuffed marinated olives,
as above

12 red pickled cocktail onions

12 cocktail skewers, e.g. brass

Cut the cheese into 12 × 2 cm (¾ in) cubes, or the size that best matches the olives. — Place the onions, olives and cheese on a lined tray, keeping them separate. — Thread the cheese first, then the olive, then the pickled onion onto each skewer. — Store in an airtight container lined with paper towel, at room temperature. — To serve, arrange all 12 skewers on a platter in the centre of the table.

Potato tart with red leicester, coriander seeds

PREP AHEAD
Toast spices and store.

DAY BEFORE
Relax.

ON THE DAY
AM
Thaw pastry in refrigerator.

PM
Make and bake tart.

Mmm ... potato, and melting cheese, and creamy mascarpone, on crisp, golden pastry? Heaven. Make this once, and you will make it forever more, experimenting with different spices and herbs, or changing the cheese, for something different. This is ridiculously good with freshly shaved truffles over the top, when in season.

CORIANDER AND THYME SALT

1 tablespoon Indian coriander seeds
1 teaspoon sea salt
2 tablespoons lemon thyme leaves

Toast the coriander seeds in a dry frying pan over a low–medium heat until fragrant and aromatic. — Remove to a mortar and pestle, then add the salt and lightly crush. — Lightly chop the thyme leaves with a knife, not too finely. — Mix together and set aside.

POTATO TART

2 × 170 g (6 oz) sheets puff pastry, around 24 cm (9½ in) square
120 g (4½ oz) mascarpone cheese
50 g (1¾ oz) red leicester cheese or cheddar, grated
sea salt and freshly milled black pepper
850 g (1 lb 14 oz), roughly 14 chat or baby coliban potatoes
50 ml (1¾ fl oz) olive oil
Coriander and thyme salt, as above

Heat the oven to 220°C (430°F). — Place two heavy duty baking trays on the middle shelf of the oven and heat for at least 30 minutes. — Cut two sheets of baking paper, around 30 × 30 cm (12 × 12 in), and place on a benchtop. — Place one sheet of puff pastry on each sheet of baking paper. — 'Dock' the puff pastry by pricking it all over with a fork. — Divide and spread the mascarpone evenly over both pastry bases in a thin layer. — Scatter the grated cheese on top, then season with sea salt and pepper. — Trim the ends from each potato and, using a mandoline, finely slice the potatoes into a bowl. Do not wash or rinse the potatoes. — Starting from one side, arrange the potatoes in lines on top of the cheese so that they overlap by about half a slice, making sure you take them right up to the edge of the pastry. — Slide the baking paper with the pastry onto cold trays and refrigerate for around 30 minutes to chill. — When chilled, drizzle with olive oil and season well with the coriander and thyme salt. — Slide the baking paper and pastry onto the preheated trays in the oven and bake for about 15 minutes. — Remove the paper from beneath the tarts and rotate 180 degrees, then bake for a further 5–10 minutes, until crisp and golden. — Remove the tarts from the oven and cool on wire racks. — To serve, flash the tarts in the oven for 2 minutes at 200°C (390°F), placed directly on the oven racks. — Cut into triangles or squares and serve.

White bean peanut butter hummus, Greek salad

As a chef, I try not to make mistakes, but sometimes a mistake can turn out to be the best thing that could have happened. When I thought I was opening a tin of chickpeas and it turned out to be white beans instead, I wasn't sure what would happen, but the combination of the creamy beans and peanut butter is quite extraordinary. Now I make it like this all the time. Embrace your mistakes, I say.

CHEF'S TIP

The natural ground peanut butter from health food stores is perfect for this.

WHITE BEAN PEANUT BUTTER HUMMUS

480 g (1 lb 1 oz) drained white beans, and 20 ml (¾ fl oz) of their liquid reserved

50 ml (1¾ fl oz) lemon juice

100 g (3½ oz) chunky peanut butter

½ garlic clove, minced

1 teaspoon cumin seeds, toasted and ground

1 teaspoon salt

50 ml (1¾ fl oz) extra-virgin olive oil

MAKES 680 G (1½ LB)

In a food processor, combine the white beans and reserved liquid, lemon juice, peanut butter, garlic and cumin and blend for 1–2 minutes, scraping down the sides every so often. — Add salt and olive oil, blending. — Scrape the hummus into an airtight container and hold at room temperature if serving that day, otherwise refrigerate until required.

GREEK SALAD

100 g (3½ oz) baby roma (plum) tomatoes, chopped

100 g (3½ oz) Lebanese (short) cucumbers, diced

100 g (3½ oz) red onion, chopped

70 g (2½ oz) kalamata olives, pitted and chopped

sea salt and freshly milled black pepper

1 teaspoon red-wine vinegar, e.g. Forvm merlot

1 teaspoon extra-virgin olive oil

In a large bowl, mix the tomatoes, cucumbers, onion and olives together, then season with salt and pepper. — Dress with the red-wine vinegar and olive oil to taste.

TO SERVE

White bean peanut butter hummus, as above

Greek salad, as above

60 g (2 oz) marinated feta, crumbled

½ bunch (20 g/¾ oz) oregano, picked

1 tablespoon sumac

6 pita breads, store bought

Spoon the white bean peanut butter hummus onto a serving plate, then use the back of a spoon to spread it over the plate. — Spoon the Greek salad onto three-quarters of the hummus, leaving some visible, and drizzle with olive oil. — Scatter feta and oregano over the top, then dust with sumac. — Toast the pitta breads on the barbecue, then cut in half and serve on the side.

CHEF'S TIP

Buy your tomatoes a week in advance to give them time to ripen, and serve them at room temperature.

If you can't find sumac, use roasted and ground cumin instead.

Peas, please!

FROM THE PANTRY
Mushroom stock
(Basics, page 220)

PREP AHEAD
Make mushroom stock
and freeze.

DAY BEFORE
Roast shallots and refrigerate.

ON THE DAY
AM
Blanch peas and refrigerate.

PM
Make miso and
mushroom butter.

Whenever we are at home discussing what to cook for dinner, one of us will usually pipe up with, 'Peas, please!' Freshly podded peas are one of the great joys of life, especially when combined with sweet, silky, roasted shallots. Add the rich creaminess of mushroom and miso butter, scented with truffle, and you have one very delicious dish.

Serving with extra truffle is, of course, optional. You can use truffle in its fresh or dried form, or as truffle paste or truffle salt.

ROASTED SHALLOTS

6 large banana shallots, unpeeled
50 ml (1¾ fl oz) olive oil
6 sprigs (30 g/1 oz) thyme
freshly milled black pepper
sea salt

Heat the oven to 185°C (365°F). — Take a large sheet of aluminium foil and line the inside of a roasting dish, allowing enough foil to overhang the dish on each side. — Put the unpeeled shallots in the centre of the foil and pour over the olive oil, thyme, pepper and salt, mixing well to coat. — Bring up the sides of the foil to enclose the shallots, and seal like a parcel. — Bake for 1 hour, or until the shallots are tender. — Remove from the oven and allow to cool. — Once cool, carefully peel away the skins, leaving the shallots whole. — Refrigerate in an airtight container until required.

BLANCHED PEAS

1 kg (2 lb 3 oz) fresh peas in their pods

Pod the peas and discard the pods in your compost bin. — Bring a large, heavy-based pot of salted water to the boil. — Meanwhile, set up a bowl of iced water, ready to refresh the peas once blanched. — When the water is boiling, cook the peas for around 45 seconds to 1 minute. — Drain immediately, then plunge the peas into the iced water. — Leave until completely cold, then drain. — Refrigerate in an airtight container lined with paper towel until required.

MISO AND MUSHROOM BUTTER

300 ml (10 fl oz) Mushroom stock (Basics, page 220)
100 g (3½ oz) Saikyo miso paste
80 g (2¾ oz) unsalted butter, diced and chilled
1 teaspoon truffle paste
sea salt, as truffle salt

MAKES 500 ML (17 FL OZ)

Pour the mushroom stock into a small, heavy-based saucepan and bring to a simmer. — Turn down the heat and whisk in the miso paste until fully incorporated. — Add the diced butter and truffle paste, and blitz with a hand-held blender until fully combined, light and airy. — Season with a little sea salt or truffle salt, and set aside.

TO SERVE

Roasted shallots, as above
1 tablespoon olive oil
50 g (1¾ oz) unsalted butter
Blanched peas, as above
sea salt or truffle salt
Mushroom and miso butter, as above
fresh or dried truffles, to serve (optional)

Heat the oven to 70°C (160°F). — Put the shallots in a small roasting tray, drizzle with the olive oil and heat in the oven for 15 minutes. — Heat a non-stick frying pan or sauté pan over a medium–high heat, then add the butter. — Once the butter melts and begins to bubble, add the peas and sauté for around 1 minute. — Add 2 tablespoons of water and bring to a simmer, seasoning with sea salt or truffle salt. — Once the peas are warm all the way through, drain off the liquid. — In a separate saucepan, bring the mushroom and miso butter to a simmer, then blitz with a hand-held blender until light and foamy. — Put the warm shallots in a serving dish, then spoon over the mushroom and miso butter to cover. — Spoon the peas over the top. Shower with truffle, if using, and serve hot.

CHEF'S TIP
When you buy fresh peas in the pod, you'll end up with half that weight in peas, e.g. 1 kg (2 lb 3 oz) peas in pod will give you 500 g (1 lb 2 oz) podded peas, enough for six.

Eggplant rotolo

A stunning dish for vegetarians and non-vegetarians alike, this has the added advantage of being assembled ahead of time. The caponata, a rich Sicilian mix of eggplant (aubergine), onions, capsicums (bell peppers) and tomatoes, can be made a few days in advance. You can put the rotolo together during the day and bake it once your guests arrive, or bake earlier and then warm through to serve.

Caponata traditionally contains olives. This one doesn't, but you can add them if you like.

FROM THE PANTRY

Marinated bullhorn peppers
(Basics, page 219)

Fragrant chilli oil
(Basics, page 216)

Essential red sauce
(Basics, page 216)

DAY BEFORE

Make the caponata
and refrigerate.

ON THE DAY

Cook the lasagne sheets.

Assemble pasta and caponata
and refrigerate.

Bake prior to guests arriving;
reheat to serve.

ROASTED EGGPLANT

3 × 250 g (9 oz)
eggplant (aubergine)

200 ml (7 fl oz) olive oil

Trim off the ends of each eggplant and cut lengthways into four long slices around 1.5 cm (½ in) thick. — Cut each slice into strips, and then into squares around 1.5 cm (½ in) wide. — Heat 2–3 tablespoons of the oil in a heavy-based skillet or non-stick frying pan. — Add just enough diced eggplant to cover the base of the pan; be careful not to overcrowd the pan. — Sauté until golden brown on all sides, adding more oil if necessary. The oil will initially get soaked up by the eggplant, but will leak out as it starts to caramelise. — Once caramelised, drain the eggplant into a sieve and place onto a tray lined with paper towel. — Repeat the process in batches, with the remaining eggplant and oil.

CAPONATA

180 g (6½ oz) Marinated
bullhorn peppers (Basics,
page 219), or Navarrico
roasted piquillo peppers

40 ml (1¼ fl oz) olive oil

2 large red onions, finely diced

3 garlic cloves, grated
on a Microplane

2 tablespoons thyme, leaves
picked and chopped

1 teaspoon Fragrant chilli oil
(Basics, page 216), optional

90 ml (3 fl oz) red-wine vinegar,
e.g. Forvm cabernet sauvignon

caramelised eggplant
(aubergine), as above

sea salt and freshly milled
black pepper

220 g (8 oz) Essential red sauce
(Basics, page 216)

MAKES 1 KG (2 LB 3 OZ)

Cut the bullhorn peppers into 1 cm (½ in) dice, then set aside. — Heat a large, heavy-based pot and add the olive oil. — Once the oil is hot but not smoking, add the red onion and garlic, and sauté until tender and lightly caramelised. — Add the thyme and chilli oil, if using, and continue to sauté for a further minute. — Deglaze the pan with the vinegar, then simmer until the vinegar has almost all evaporated. — Add the bullhorn peppers and eggplant to the pan, tossing well to combine. — Season well with salt and pepper, then add the essential red sauce and bring to a simmer. — Cook for a few minutes until well combined, then pour into a container and allow to cool.

PASTA

15 dried lasagne sheets, 20 × 5 cm
(8 × 2 in) (about 500 g/1 lb 2 oz in
total), e.g. Afeltra ruffled lasagne

In a 12 litre (405 fl oz) pot, cook the pasta in plenty of boiling salted water until al dente – it needs to be flexible enough to roll up. — If you don't have a large enough pot, cook the sheets in two batches, otherwise they may break up. — Refresh in cold running water and pat dry, then select the 12 best sheets to use.

CHEF'S TIP

Look for smaller eggplants
(aubergines), around 250 g
(9 oz) each, as they will be firmer
and have less water content.
Larger ones are spongier and
will absorb more oil.

Look for ruffled lasagne sheets
from Italian producer Afeltra –
they're the perfect shape
and size (20 × 5 cm/8 × 2 in)
for rotolo.

ROTOLOS

200 g (7 oz) Essential red sauce (Basics, page 216)	
cooked lasagne sheets, page 160	
Caponata, page 160	
180 g (6½ oz) fontina cheese, grated	
180 g (6½ oz) mozzarella cheese, grated	
1 bunch basil leaves, picked	

Spoon the essential red sauce into the bottom of a 22 × 4 cm (8¾×1½in)highceramicbakingdish.—Workinginanorderlyfashion, lay the lasagne sheets vertically in front of you on the benchtop. — Spread roughly 80 g (2¾ oz) of caponata over the pasta, up to 2 cm (¾ in) from the end. — Spread about 15 g (½ oz) each of fontina and mozzarella evenly on top. — Add a few basil leaves, then roll up the pasta to encase the filling. — Stand the rotolo in the prepared baking dish, making sure that it does not unroll. — Repeat with the remaining 11 rotolos, fitting them snugly into the baking dish. — Cover with plastic wrap and refrigerate until ready to bake.

TO BAKE AND SERVE

Rotolos, as above	
30 ml (1 fl oz) olive oil	
50 g (1¾ oz) mozzarella cheese, grated	

Heat the oven to 180°C (360°F). — Remove the rotolos from the refrigerator and discard the plastic wrap. — Drizzle with olive oil, then cover with aluminium foil and bake for 30 minutes. — At this stage, remove the foil and scatter the rotolos with mozzarella cheese. — Bake for a further 15 minutes, until the pasta is crisp and the cheese has melted. — Allow to cool slightly before serving. — Drizzle with a little olive oil and serve in the centre of the table, allowing your guests to help themselves.

SERVES 6

Butternut, burrata, roasted chilli

FROM THE PANTRY
Taberu rayu table chilli (Basics, page 226)

ON THE DAY
Roast butternut.

The humble butternut pumpkin (squash) is a paid-up member of the cucurbits family, much-loved for its sweet, nutty flavour. But it's when the natural sugars caramelise in the roasting that it really shines – especially when coated with a beautiful Japanese table chilli, and served with gooey, creamy-hearted burrata cheese nestled in its hollows. The combined effect of sweetness, spice and creaminess is tantalising.

CHEF'S TIP
A quick shortcut is to buy your butternut pumpkin in two separate halves – that way, there's no need to split a whole one.

1 large butternut pumpkin (squash), 1.8–2 kg (4 lb–4 lb 6 oz), split in two	
50 ml (1¾ fl oz) olive oil	
sea salt and freshly milled black pepper	
100 g (3½ oz) Taberu rayu table chilli (Basics, page 226)	
2 fresh burrata cheeses	

Heat oven to 190°C (375°F). — Using a tablespoon, remove the seeds from the centres of both butternut halves, and discard. — Score the flesh side of the butternut in a criss-cross manner, then rub with olive oil and season heavily with salt and pepper. — Bake cut-side up for around 45–50 minutes. — Remove the butternut halves to a wire rack. — Spoon the taberu rayu table chilli onto the flesh side to coat well, then return to the oven. — Bake for a further 20 minutes or until soft and caramelised. — Meanwhile, drain the burrata on paper towel. — To serve, place the butternut onto a serving platter. — Put a burrata in each butternut hollow, drizzle with a little more taberu rayu, and serve.

Coconut rice, maraschino cherries, shaved chocolate

If you're thinking rice pudding is a bit of a nanna dish, think again. Enriched with coconut cream and swirled with the tang of sour cherries, this is a very adult version of a childhood favourite, right down to the bitterness of the dark chocolate on top.

If you make the rice ahead and refrigerate, it will become quite thick and creamy – just adjust the consistency with a little extra cold milk. Luxardo cherries in their own syrup are a blessing to have in the pantry – they last forever and are brilliant with ice cream, as well as in fruit cakes, tarts and puddings (and especially in one of our favourite cocktails, The Last Word).

CREAMED RICE

95 g (3¼ oz) jasmine rice
220 g (8 oz) thickened (whipping) cream
300 ml (10 fl oz) full-cream milk
400 g (14 oz) coconut cream
½ teaspoon vanilla paste
65 g (2¼ oz) caster (superfine) sugar
8 whole green cardamon pods

MAKES 900 G (2 LB)

Put all the ingredients in a heavy-based casserole dish or saucepan and bring to the boil, stirring. — As soon as the mixture boils, turn the heat to the lowest setting and let the rice cook gently for around 40 minutes until thick and creamy. — Stir every couple of minutes, so that it does not stick to the base of the pan and burn. — Once cooked, remove the cardamon pods and then pour the rice into a container. — Place a sheet of baking paper on top to stop a skin from forming, and allow to cool, then cover and refrigerate until required.

CHOCOLATE ORANGE

180 g (6½ oz) block of dark chocolate (70%)
2 blood or navel oranges

Coarsely grate the chocolate into a bowl using a box grater. — Zest the orange directly into the chocolate, folding it through to stop it clumping. — Refrigerate in an airtight container until required.

TO SERVE

Creamed rice, as above
150–180 g (5½–6½ oz) thickened (whipping) cream, chilled
400 g (14 oz) Luxardo maraschino cherries in syrup
1 glazed maraschino cherry, for garnish (optional)

Pour the creamed rice into a bowl and add a little fresh cream to make it nice and creamy. — Pour the rice into a glass serving bowl around 18 cm (7 in) in diameter and 10 cm (4 in) high. — Pour the Luxardo maraschino cherries and syrup over the rice, covering it completely. — Scatter with chocolate orange to cover, and place a glazed maraschino cherry on top if you like. — Serve in the centre of the table, and let your guests help themselves.

CHEF'S TIP
In winter, serve the rice warm, with a scoop of vanilla ice cream and a shaving of chocolate over the top, and watch how it all melts together into rice pudding heaven.

8 THE SUNSET SOIREE

ALL DISHES **SERVED TOGETHER** **BUFFET STYLE**	Oysters, lime and rice-wine vinegar Crudités, crab mayonnaise Barbecued scallops, black bean and blood orange Pancetta prawns, mint yoghurt, smoked oil Barbecued marrons, preserved lemon, Sichuan pepper Grilled octopus, kipflers, chilli crunch
DESSERT	Champagne and raspberry jellies
WINE TIME	Ultra Brut Champagne Austrian dry grüner veltliner Provençal-style rosé Light and fresh gamay Demi-Sec Champagne (*best served in white wine glasses*)
COCKTAIL HOUR	Sunset Lillet Rosé 211

A dinner party can, and should, take many forms. Getting together with friends doesn't always have to be a night-time affair. That's why I love the idea of a sunset soiree.

It's a dinner party that happens on a Sunday afternoon, when everyone has already had a great weekend, but can still find a few hours to pop over for a few drinks and some amazing seafood grilled on the barbecue, out in the fresh air.

It's easy, leisurely and celebratory. Monday is another day, and there's no pressure for anyone to be on their best behaviour – which is probably just as well. And if you have a pool, it's quite likely that everyone will end up taking a dip.

The best thing about the sunset soiree is that you have all Sunday morning to get everything ready, so you'll be as relaxed as your guests are. And once the sun has set over the horizon, that's the signal for everyone to drift off into the night, and you get the rest of the evening to yourself.

Or at least, that's the plan. One spectacular weekend, our guests didn't leave until the wee hours of the morning, so good luck with that.

I've based this menu around the best of Australia's abundant, sustainable seafood, and mixed in some dips and snacks to keep everyone happy.

With the morning's prep under your belt, you can welcome your guests, pour a drink, have an oyster or some crisp crudités with crab mayo, and then wander off to cook the seafood. There's nothing more beautifully Australian than hovering over the grill, tongs in one hand and a spritz or a beer in the other, laughing and joking with friends on a sunny Sunday afternoon.

While the scallops, prawns (shrimp), marrons or octopus all cook relatively quickly, I've teamed them with some racy little accompaniments and dressings that will be ready to go when you are. It's a way of eating that suits the occasion; relaxed and accommodating. For that reason, I favour a light and summery dessert, such as a champagne and raspberry jelly that's vibrant, pink and bubbly, but not too sweet.

It's a grazing menu, so just set up a central table for the food and invite everyone to help themselves. Put out all the glasses, plates, cutlery and napkins to promote the idea of self-service, but note: this isn't a buffet, it's a soiree. Big difference!

THE PLAYLIST **THE BAMBOOS** 4 **BEN E. KING** Supernatural Thing **BOOZOO BAJOU** Sat Keep Watching the Stars **DEAD COMBO** Lisboa Mulata **FRANK OCEAN** Blond **LA ROU THE CENTURIONS** Bullwinkle Part II

LUR The Magic Whip **CHANCHA VIA CIRCUITO** Bienaventuranza **CLELIA FELIX**
upervision **RAY BARRETTO** Charanga Moderna **TIM LOVE LEE** Against Remixes

Oysters, lime and rice-wine vinegar

FROM THE PANTRY
Lime and rice-wine vinegar
(Basics, page 219)

ON THE DAY
Open oysters.

When it comes to oysters, my advice is that if you can open them yourself, you should, which is why I've given a really explicit guide here. Oysters are at their best when freshly opened and swimming in salty juices. Buying them unopened is also the best way to purchase and transport them, as they will maintain the liquid salinity that keeps them fresh.

This fresh, zingy dressing has been a key recipe of mine since 2004. I created it because traditional vinaigrettes such as shallot and red-wine vinegar can be too strong and acidic for the delicate taste and texture of an oyster. Rice-wine vinegar is softer, and with the addition of lime juice and its oily zest, it 'wakes up' the taste of the oyster instead of masking it. Use it for other seafood also, such as kingfish or squid.

TO OPEN OYSTERS

3 teaspoons sea salt

400 ml (13½ fl oz) cold water

24 rock or Pacific oysters

Make a saltwater solution by mixing the salt and water, stirring until the salt is dissolved. This will be used to wash any shell grit from the oysters without ruining their natural sea-saltiness. — To open the oysters, you will require an oyster knife and a tea towel (dish towel). This takes some practice, and you will get better over time. Do not try to open oysters with an ordinary knife, as it is very dangerous. — Under running water, wash each oyster of any sand, grit or mud that may be on the outside of the shell. — Dampen the tea towel and fold lengthways into thirds. — Set the oyster curved side down, flat side up, on the folded towel. If you are right-handed, position the oyster so that its hinge (where the shells taper together) is pointing to the right. — Fold the towel over the oyster so that only the hinge is exposed and place your non-dominant hand on top to hold it steady. Try to bunch up the folded towel in front of that hand. If the oyster knife slips, the towel will be the only thing protecting your hand. — Work the point of your oyster knife into the hinge between the two shells. — Once you have some leverage, push the knife into the gap and move it left and right, up and down, applying a little pressure. — This isn't about forcing the knife between the shells, it's about finesse. Wiggle the knife around until you feel like you can exert some pressure against both the top and bottom shells at once by twisting and prying the knife. — As you angle your knife, you should be pushing it in an upwards motion until you hear a pop and the shells part. — Once the shells have popped apart you will have a narrow opening. Now you need to break the muscle that holds the shells together. — To do this, press the flat side of the knife hard up against the flat side of the top shell and run it along, breaking the muscle and separating the two shells. — Discard the top shell, then run the oyster knife under the muscle to release the oyster from the shell. — Flip the oyster over within the bottom shell. Use a brush dipped in the saltwater solution to brush away any shell that may have broken off.

TO SERVE

250 ml (8½ fl oz) Lime and rice-wine vinegar (Basics, page 221)

lemon wedges

Arrange the shucked oysters on a platter and serve with the dressing on the side, and lemon wedges if desired.

CHEF'S TIP
Once opened, do not rinse the oysters in water, as you will wash away their distinct flavour.

Crudités, crab mayonnaise

DAY BEFORE

Cook crab and make
crab mayonnaise.

Prep vegetables and store.

ON THE DAY

Chop tarragon and mix
with crab mayonnaise.

Dips are back, baby, and they're here to stay. This is a play on the crudités made famous by the dinner parties of the 1970s, now referred to by the glorious name 'chips and dips'.

To make this more luxurious, I've added a stunning spanner crab mayonnaise. Prepping the vegetables for the crudités takes a little time, but can be done the day before if you store them in airtight containers lined with damp paper towel. Then on the day, all you need to do is slip into your soiree gear, plate up and serve.

TO PREPARE CRABMEAT

250 g (9 oz) spanner crabmeat, raw (or any white crabmeat)	
50 g (1¾ oz) unsalted butter	

Put the crabmeat in a sieve over a bowl and cover with plastic wrap. — Refrigerate for 2 hours to allow excess water to drain from the crab. — Place the drained crabmeat on a tray and check that there is no shell within the meat. — Heat the butter in a wide, heavy-based saucepan a over low–medium heat. — Once bubbling, add the crabmeat and toss gently in the butter for a minute or two, being careful not to break up the delicate meat, until just cooked. — Drain the crab in a sieve set over a bowl, to remove the excess butter. — Set aside and cool at room temperature.

CITRUS AND TARRAGON MAYONNAISE

100 g (3½ oz) Kewpie (QP) or whole egg mayonnaise	
60 g (2 oz) crème fraîche or sour cream	
zest of 1 lemon	
1 tablespoon lemon juice	
pinch of cayenne pepper	
40 g (1½ oz, about 1 bunch) tarragon, leaves picked and lightly chopped	

In a bowl, add the mayonnaise, crème fraîche, lemon zest and juice and cayenne, and whisk until smooth. — Add the tarragon just before serving.

CRUDITÉS

12 baby Dutch purple carrots	
12 baby Dutch orange carrots	
6 baby cucumbers	
12 red belle radishes, with stalks	
12 asparagus	
3 celery stalks	
12 spring onions (scallions)	
2 witlof (Belgian endive)	

Wash the carrots then scrub with a clean scourer, cleaning any soil around the stems. — Cut the cucumbers into long batons. — Wash the radishes in iced water and clean the leaves around the top, removing any imperfect leaves. Cut the radishes into halves or quarters, depending on size. — Snap each asparagus stalk and discard the woody end. Peel the remaining stem if required to remove any stringy fibres. — Trim the celery into 12 cm (4¾ in) batons, using a peeler to remove the stringy parts. — Trim the roots and tops of the spring onions (scallions). — Place all prepared vegetables on a tray lined with damp paper towel, then cover and refrigerate until required. — Separate the witlof leaves and select the nice even middle leaves. Refrigerate in an airtight container until required.

TO SERVE

Crudités, as above	
cooked crabmeat, as above	
Citrus and tarragon mayonnaise, as above	

Set up a chip-and-dip plate, or a platter with a bowl in the centre. — Arrange the crudités neatly around the outside, alternating the colours. — Fold the cooked crabmeat through the mayonnaise, and season to taste. — Spoon the crab mayonnaise into the bowl, or the centre of the platter, and serve immediately.

Barbecued scallops, black bean and blood orange

FROM THE PANTRY
Seasoned rice-wine vinegar
(Basics, page 224)

DAY BEFORE
Make blood orange and
black bean dressing.
Prep scallops and refrigerate.

The thing I love about scallops is that the shells are the perfect vehicles to carry flavour directly to the scallops' briny, slightly sweet, buttery flesh. You can buy farmed scallops on the half shell all year round in Australia, with wild scallops in season from September to December. Just make sure that you don't overcook them, so they stay succulent and tender, rather than turn spongy and dry.

BLOOD ORANGE AND BLACK BEAN DRESSING

4 blood oranges
2 tablespoons salted black beans, finely chopped
50 ml (1¾ fl oz) Seasoned rice-wine vinegar (Basics, page 224)
50 ml (1¾ fl oz) olive oil

Zest the blood oranges, then juice them. You will need 300 ml (10 fl oz) blood orange juice. — Put the zest and the chopped black beans in a bowl. — Pour the blood orange juice into a heavy-based saucepan and bring to the boil. — Simmer and reduce by two-thirds, until you have 100 ml (3½ fl oz) juice. — Pour the hot reduced blood orange juice over the zest and black beans, and allow to sit for 2 minutes. — Add vinegar, tossing well, then whisk in the olive oil. — Pour into an airtight container and set aside.

SCALLOPS

24 scallops, in the half shell

Clean the scallops using damp paper towel to help remove any sand from around the shell. — Transfer to a container and seal with a lid, then refrigerate until required.

TO SERVE

scallops, as above
2 tablespoons extra-virgin olive oil
sea salt and freshly milled black pepper
Blood orange and black bean dressing, as above

Heat the barbecue to high, and close the lid. — Arrange the scallops on a tray. Brush each one with a little olive oil and season with salt and pepper. — Place on the grill flesh-side up and cook over the high heat for 2 minutes, until you hear the scallop meat 'pop' and it looks translucent. — Remove from the heat and place on the tray. — Mix the blood orange and black bean dressing with a whisk, then spoon a tablespoon of dressing over each scallop, to just coat. — Place onto a serving platter in the centre of the table.

CHEF'S TIP
Blood oranges are quite spectacular, but their season is quite short (August to October), so feel free to replace with navel or valencia oranges.

Pancetta prawns, mint yoghurt, smoked oil

FROM THE PANTRY
Korean-style chilli paste
(Basics, page 218)

DAY BEFORE
Wrap prawns in bacon and store.
Make yoghurt and mint dip.

These prawns (shrimp) are dressed for the occasion in smoky little pancetta waistcoats, ready to dip into creamy, minty yoghurt. The smoked olive oil adds another dimension, and the yoghurt cools off any spicy heat. Get them sizzling on the barbecue when your guests arrive, and let that sweet, smoky smell bring them to the table.

PANCETTA-WRAPPED PRAWNS

18 raw banana prawns (shrimp), green (size 31/40)

2 tablespoons Korean-style chilli paste or gochujang paste (Basics, page 218)

18 thin slices of smoked pancetta, 20 cm (8 in) long

Peel the prawns, leaving the tail ends intact (freeze the heads and shells to make shellfish oil another time). — Run a small, sharp knife down the backs of the prawns to remove the intestinal tract and discard. — Place the prawns on a tray lined with paper towel. Cover with more paper towel and refrigerate for a couple of hours. — Remove the prawns from the refrigerator and discard the paper towel. — Lay the prawns out on the tray and brush all over with the Korean chilli paste until lightly coated. — Lay a strip of pancetta on the bench vertically in front of you. — Put a prawn at the bottom of the pancetta strip, with the tail to one side of the pancetta, and roll up to wrap and encase the prawn. — Pass a wooden skewer into the tail end of the prawn and through the centre, right to the top, to keep the prawn straight and secure the pancetta in place. — Repeat with the remaining prawns. — Lay six of the skewered prawns side by side. Using two additional skewers, push one skewer through the head end and the other through the tail end of the prawns, securing all six prawns together – this makes it very easy to turn them on the grill. Repeat with the remaining prawns, so you have three groups of six. — Return the prawns to the tray and refrigerate until required.

MINT YOGHURT

200 g (7 oz) Greek yoghurt

zest of 1 lemon

60 g (2 oz/about 2 bunches) mint, leaves picked

MAKES 230 G (8 OZ)

Put the yoghurt in a bowl and stir in the lemon zest. — Place the mint leaves on a cutting board. Bunching them together in one hand, shred the leaves into fine strips with a sharp knife, then add to the yoghurt and stir through. — Refrigerate in an airtight container until required.

TO SERVE

prepared prawns, as above

Mint yoghurt, as above

2 tablespoons smoked olive oil, store bought

Heat the barbecue to high, and close the lid. — Once the barbecue is hot, grill the prawns for around 1-2 minutes on each side until caramelised and crisp. — Place on a tray and keep warm. — Spoon the minted yoghurt into a bowl on a serving platter. — Remove the two skewers holding each group of prawns together, then arrange the prawns around the bowl. — Make an indentation in the centre of the yoghurt with the back of a spoon and pour in the smoked olive oil. — Serve immediately.

CHEF'S TIP
Hitting the prawns with a high heat from the start will make sure the pancetta renders and crisps up beautifully. The prawns will cook quickly, but if you take them straight from the refrigerator, the centre will take that bit longer to cook, as the pancetta crisps.

Barbecued marrons, preserved lemon, Sichuan pepper

Seasoned rice-wine vinegar
(Basics, page 224)

Shellfish oil (Basics, page 225)

DAY BEFORE
Store marrons in cold,
dark conditions.

ON THE DAY
Dispatch marrons
and refrigerate.

Make preserved lemon
butter sauce.

Sometimes you have to wow your guests with something very special – and marrons will do that every time. The international chefs I've worked with envy me for being able to work with this beautifully sweet delicacy in Australia. Now farmed in Western Australia and South Australia, marron is more easily available, although still not cheap.

Buy the marrons live, as they lose their freshness quite rapidly once killed. If that's not for you, then consider bugs (flat-head lobster), rock lobster, scampi, or large (size U6) prawns (shrimp) instead, though cooking times will vary.

THE MARRONS

6 × 200 g (7 oz) marrons, live

Live marrons can be quite lively, so it is best to keep them as cold as possible, and in a dark place, as soon as you get them. — To prepare them for cooking, first dampen two tea towels (dish towels) and chill in the freezer for around 10 minutes. — To dispatch the marrons, put them in the freezer for 30 minutes. — Lay the first tea towel onto the base of a roasting tray or container large enough to hold the marrons. — Put a cutting board next to the sink so that any liquids can be washed away. — Working with one marron at a time, place the marron onto the cutting board and pierce a sharp knife between the eyes and the centre of the head. — Using a large, solid knife, cut the marron in half lengthways by placing the knife in the cut already made, and cutting all the way through the head. — Turn the marron around and cut through the tail so that you have two halves. — Clean out the head cavity and remove the intestinal tract, then place the marron on the tea-towel lined tray. — Repeat with the remaining marrons, then cover with the second wet tea towel and refrigerate until required.

PRESERVED LEMON BUTTER SAUCE

3 shallots, finely diced

100 ml (3½ fl oz) Seasoned rice-wine vinegar (Basics, page 225)

100 ml (3½ fl oz) lemon juice

150 ml (5 fl oz) sake or white wine

100 g (3½ oz) thickened (whipping) cream

200 g (7 oz) butter, diced

50 g (1¾ oz) preserved lemon, cleaned and chopped

zest of 2 lemons

MAKES 500 G (1 LB 2 OZ)

In a heavy-based saucepan, combine the shallots, vinegar and lemon juice and bring to a simmer. — Allow to simmer and reduce until it is syrupy and almost evaporated, being careful not to let it caramelise. — Add the sake or wine, and reduce again until almost evaporated. — Add the cream and bring to the boil, then turn down the heat and slowly whisk in the diced butter, a few cubes at a time, until incorporated. Do not boil the sauce. — Once all the butter has been added, remove from the heat. — Add the preserved lemon and lemon zest and blitz with a hand-held blender until smooth and creamy. Keep warm until required.

TO SERVE

6 prepared marrons, as above

50 ml (1¾ fl oz) Shellfish oil (Basics, page 225)

1 teaspoon salt

2 tablespoons Sichuan peppercorns, toasted and crushed

Preserved lemon butter sauce, as above

pinch of Aleppo chilli flakes

Heat the barbecue to high, and close the lid. — Brush the marrons with a little shellfish oil and season well with salt and Sichuan peppercorns. — Once the barbecue is hot enough, place the marrons on the grill shell-side down, and grill for 3–4 minutes until the flesh turns opaque. — Arrange on a platter and spoon over the preserved lemon butter sauce, reserving some to serve. — Drizzle over the remaining shellfish oil and season with Aleppo chilli flakes. — Serve with the remaining preserved lemon butter sauce on the side.

CHEF'S NOTE
Cooking the marrons in the half shell gives a lovely smokiness to the flesh. When you see the meat turning white from the outside to the almost translucent centre, they're cooked.

Grilled octopus, kipflers, chilli crunch

FROM THE PANTRY

Seasoned rice-wine vinegar
(Basics, page 224)

Kabayaki sauce
(Basics, page 217)

Crispy rayu chilli
(Basics, page 215)

DAY BEFORE

Braise the octopus
a few days prior.

Make lemon and shallot
dressing and refrigerate.

ON THE DAY

Cook potatoes 3 hours prior.

Most people have their first experience of eating octopus when dining out, but it's great to cook at home, especially on a barbecue. I have always been fascinated with cephalopods, from octopus to cuttlefish and squid. Not only are they a joy to cook, but you can buy them in advance and freeze them, which helps tenderise the flesh. Alternatively purchase already frozen.

For me, the Portuguese and Japanese are the most expert octopus cooks, so I have based this recipe on the Portuguese dish of *polvo grelhado com batatas* (grilled octopus with potatoes), then mixed in a little Japanese magic with a sweet soy glaze and crispy rayu chilli.

TO BRAISE THE OCTOPUS

1 kg (2 lb 3 oz) octopus tentacles, heads and innards removed (around 6–8 tentacles from a large octopus)

5 garlic cloves

30 g (1 oz) thyme

1 tablespoon peppercorns, crushed

130 g (4½ oz) kalamata olives, 100 ml (3½ fl oz) of their brine reserved

zest and juice of 2 oranges

150 ml (5 fl oz) white soy sauce

350 ml (12 fl oz) white wine (e.g. riesling)

150 ml (5 fl oz) olive oil

Place a 6 litre (203 fl oz) heavy-based pot on the stove and fill two-thirds full with cold water. — Bring to a rolling boil. — Meanwhile, clean the octopus under cold running water. Rinse well and drain. — Once the water is boiling, add the octopus and blanch for around 1 minute. — Remove and rinse under cold running water, then drain. — Separate the octopus into individual tentacles. — Return to the pan and add 2.5 litres (85 fl oz) of water along with the remaining ingredients — Bring the mixture to the boil, then simmer gently for 1–1½ hours, or until the octopus is tender. — Once cooked, remove from the heat and leave in the cooking liquid to cool. — When cool, remove the octopus from the cooking liquid and put in a container large enough to hold both octopus and liquid. — Strain the cooking liquid through a fine strainer over the octopus, to cover. — Seal with a lid and refrigerate until required. You can cook this in advance and refrigerate for a few days if you prefer.

LEMON AND SHALLOT DRESSING

50 ml (1¾ fl oz) Seasoned rice-wine vinegar (Basics, page 225)

zest of 1 lemon

40 ml (1¼ fl oz) lemon juice

2 large shallots, finely diced

freshly milled black pepper

smoked salt (e.g. Olsson's)

90 ml (3 fl oz) olive oil

Put the rice-wine vinegar, lemon zest and juice, shallots, pepper and salt into a bowl and whisk until combined. — Whisk in the olive oil until smooth and emulsified, and set aside.

KIPFLER POTATOES

750 g (1 lb 11 oz) kipfler (fingerling) potatoes, all roughly the same size

Lemon and shallot dressing, as above

salt

Wash the potatoes and scrub the skins with a scourer to remove any dirt, then rinse well. — Put the potatoes in a heavy-based saucepan, then fill with water, add a good amount of salt and bring to a boil. — Simmer gently for around 30–40 minutes, or until tender, using a knife to test for doneness. — Drain the potatoes and leave until still warm, but cool enough to handle. — Use a small paring knife to peel away the skins, then slice into 2–3 cm (¾–1¼ in) thick pieces. — Put the sliced potatoes in a bowl and pour over the lemon and shallot dressing, tossing gently to combine. — Season to taste, then cover with foil or a heatproof lid and keep warm in an oven set to 50°C (120°F).

CHEF'S TIP

I prefer to buy the frozen large cleaned octopus tentacles and simply defrost in the bag under running cold water. Otherwise it pays to buy your fresh octopus a few days prior and freeze it, which helps tenderise the flesh. If you freeze it in a plastic bag, you can thaw it by running cold water over it, without washing away any flavour.

TO SERVE

prepared octopus, page 178

100 ml (3½ fl oz) Kabayaki sauce (Basics, page 217)

warm kipfler (fingerling) potatoes, (page 178)

2 tablespoons Crispy rayu chilli (Basics, page 215) or store bought

½ teaspoon smoked sweet paprika

oil for drizzling

Heat the barbecue on high, and close the lid. — Drain the octopus from the braising liquid and remove any of the loose webbed skin from the tentacles. Discard the braising liquid. — Drizzle the octopus with a little oil and grill until smoky and lightly charred. — Brush with the kabayaki sauce and grill briefly until sticky and glazed, then remove and keep warm. — Meanwhile, remove the potatoes from the oven and spoon into the centre of a high-rimmed 22 cm (8¾ in) serving plate. — Cut the octopus into manageable pieces and arrange on top of the potatoes. — Sprinkle with crispy rayu chilli, and dust with a little paprika. — Serve immediately.

Champagne and raspberry jellies

PREP AHEAD
Make raspberry syrup
a few days prior.

DAY BEFORE
Make jellies in advance, cover
with plastic wrap once set,
and refrigerate.

ON THE DAY
Serve with raspberry on top.

A Champagne and raspberry jelly in an elegant glass or coupe just screams summery good times. These are so simple to make, and super light to eat; the perfect ending to a long lunch or an early evening soiree. Consider making them two days in advance and literally forgetting about them until you pop them on a tray and bring them out.

RASPBERRY SYRUP

½ teaspoon vanilla paste

110 g (4 oz) caster (superfine) sugar

250 g (9 oz) frozen raspberries

In a small, heavy-based pot, combine 450 ml (15 fl oz) water, vanilla and sugar and bring to the boil. — Once boiled, add the frozen raspberries and return to the boil. — Remove from the heat and cover with a lid, then leave for 30 minutes to infuse. — Gently pour the syrup through a paper coffee filter into a bowl. You should obtain 500 ml (17 fl oz). If short, just top up with a little water. — Pour into an airtight container and refrigerate until required.

CHAMPAGNE AND RASPBERRY JELLIES

9 gelatine leaves, gold strength

500 ml (17 fl oz) Raspberry syrup, as above

400 ml (13½ fl oz) Champagne

6 fresh raspberries

Soak the gelatine in iced water for around 5 minutes until hydrated, then squeeze out any excess water and set aside. — Pour 100 ml (3½ fl oz) of the raspberry syrup into a saucepan and bring to the boil. — Add the gelatine and stir until dissolved. — Strain the mixture through a fine sieve into the remaining raspberry syrup. — Open the Champagne and pour yourself a glass. You deserve it. — Add 400 ml (13½ fl oz) Champagne to the raspberry syrup, stirring gently, then ladle into champagne glasses. — Refrigerate to set for at least 4–6 hours, preferably overnight. — When ready to serve, pop a raspberry on top.

CHEF'S TIP
Swap raspberries for strawberries if you prefer, or even fresh peaches for a bellini-inspired version. Top up with more Champagne if that's the mood you're in.

9 FANCY SCHMANCY

CANAPES / SNACKS
SERVED ON ARRIVAL
Oscietra caviar, créme fraîche, fried bread
Smoked salmon, creamed horseradish

STARTERS
SHARED AND SERVED
AT THE SAME TIME
Tuna, avocado, caviar
San Daniele, Corella pears, lemony pink peppercorn oil

SECOND STARTER
SERVED SEPARATELY
Crab, devilled egg, green toasts

MAINS & SIDES
SERVED TOGETHER
ON THE TABLE
Just a prime rib (*okay, with truffle*)
Straw potatoes, truffle salt
Watercress salad, go-to honey mustard dressing

DESSERT
Bitter chocolate tart, Pedro Ximénez dates

WINE TIME
Vintage Champagne (*best served in white wine glasses*)
Smooth Junmai Daiginjo sake (*best served chilled*)
Aged rose and leather piemontese nebbiolo
A red Bordeaux blend (*best decanted before serving*)
Sweet fortified red wine (*port, Pedro Ximénez*)

COCKTAIL HOUR The Dry Martini 211

Sometimes you need to pull out the big guns. The prime rib of beef. The bitter chocolate tart. It could be a big nought birthday, friends leaving town, or a meal with the sort of mates who have come to dinner before, and might be expecting an upgrade from business to first.

The idea behind this menu is not to go all out with the bells and whistles of restaurant wizardry, but rather, that a little luxury can be a very good thing. A little caviar, a little smoked salmon, a little truffle, perhaps? It's about the quality of prime ingredients, the opulence, the decadence and the indulgence of a great dinner party. It's a way of spoiling people, and making them feel special.

It could also be the right moment to crack open that wine you have had hidden under the stairs for the past 20 years. Drink it in its prime, before it turns to vinegar. Seize the day! (Okay, the night.) And have some back-up wines because there's always that one pesky person who doesn't like aged semillon.

Here's how to play the fancy-schmancy game:

Set the table with style and whimsy, using your best cutlery, glassware and ceramics, beautiful placemats, napkin rings if you have them, and ice buckets to boot.

Add a few coloured votive candles (scentless is best, so they don't affect the beautiful smell of the food), and some just-picked greenery for glamour and freshness.

Start the night right with a vintage Champagne – let's not mess about here. Or serve a cocktail on arrival, with canapés. It's a great ice-breaker (don't forget the ice!), and sets the scene for a fun and convivial night.

And do keep up the water supply throughout the evening. We're big fans of carbonating your own sparkling water instead of buying bottled water – much kinder on the environment.

Sharing food and wine with friends is one of life's great pleasures, and you have the power to make this dinner party one that will be remembered and talked about for years to come. What fun.

THE PLAYLIST **BUGGE WESSELTOFT** Everybody Loves Angels **DAVID 'FATHEAD' NEWMA** Morning **HERBIE HANCOCK** Round Midnight Soundtrack **HORACE SILVER** The Bl with You **MILES DAVIS** Ascenseur Pour L'échafaud **MULGREW MILLER** Forget Me No

he Blessing **DEXTER GORDON** Landslide Grant **GREEN GREEN** Street/Sunday
te Years **JOHN COLTRANE** Coltrane's Sound **KEITH JARRETT** The Melody at Night,
TAN GETZ AND JOÃO GILBERTO Getz/Gilberto **TINA BROOKS** True Blue

Oscietra caviar, crème fraîche, fried bread

PREP AHEAD
Buy caviar and refrigerate.

DAY BEFORE
Cut bread and store
in an airtight container.

ON THE DAY
Fry bread.

This is a super-decadent little bite to start your evening, paired with a glass of Champagne or a dry martini. The trick is to serve the fried bread warm, which heats the oils in the caviar and brings out its mouth-filling richness.

TOASTS

3 slices of white bread or milk bread, around 2 cm (¾ in) thick

400 ml (13½ fl oz) canola or vegetable oil

fine salt

TO SERVE

Toasts, as above

120 g (4½ oz) crème fraîche or sour cream

50–100 g (1¾–3½ oz) Oscietra caviar (the more the merrier)

Using a 3 cm (1¼ in) round pastry cutter, cut out 18 rounds of bread. — Heat the oil in a small, heavy-based frying pan – it should be ½ cm (¼ in) deep. — When the oil is hot, carefully fry the bread on both sides until golden, then drain on paper towel and season with fine salt. — Once cool, put in a container lined with paper towel and set aside in a cool, dry place.

Heat the oven to 50°C (120°F). — Place the toasts on a tray and heat for 10 minutes, until warm. — Top each toast with a little crème fraîche and a dollop of caviar and serve.

CHEF'S TIP
The bread will fry better if day-old rather than fresh, so cut it into the required shapes or tear into more rustic shapes the day before, and store in an airtight container.

Smoked salmon, creamed horseradish

PREP AHEAD
Buy sliced smoked salmon.

DAY BEFORE
Make smoked salmon filling.
Assemble balls and refrigerate.

ON THE DAY
Chop chives finely.

These are seriously good little bombs of flavour, inspired by a classic Sepia canapé. It may take a little time to master the technique of turning them into perfect orbs, but once made, they are simple to serve, saving you time on the night. Rolled in chives and filled with crème fraîche and horseradish, this is a traditional flavour combination seen through another lens.

SMOKED SALMON

600 g (1 lb 5 oz) smoked salmon, pre-sliced

Set out the smoked salmon and select the 14 best slices. — Trim each slice to around 8 × 8 cm (3¼ × 3¼ in), removing any brown flesh, and reserving the trimmings. — Arrange the slices in a single layer on a tray lined with plastic wrap and set aside.

SALMON MIX FILLING

120 g (4½ oz) smoked salmon trimmings, as above
45 g (1½ oz) crème fraîche or sour cream
1 heaped tablespoon strong horseradish cream (e.g. Tracklements)
freshly milled black pepper

Finely dice the salmon trimmings. — Mix the crème fraîche and horseradish cream together in a bowl, season with black pepper, and fold in the chopped salmon. — Refrigerate in an airtight container until required.

SMOKED SALMON BALLS

Smoked salmon, as above
Salmon mix filling, as above

Place one slice of smoked salmon on a board or tray. — Put one teaspoon of the salmon mix filling in the centre of the slice, then use a palette knife to flip the corners of the sliced salmon up around the filling so that it is completely covered. — Repeat with the remaining slices of salmon. — To form the salmon into perfect orbs, line the bench with a double layer of plastic wrap, around 25 × 25 cm (10 × 10 in). — Put a filled smoked salmon ball in the centre of the plastic wrap. — Gather up each corner of the plastic wrap with your fingers, shaping the salmon into a sphere, and twisting the plastic wrap to make it as tight as possible. — Put each sphere in the refrigerator as you make them, and leave to set for 2 hours or overnight. — Unmould the spheres from the plastic wrap, put them in an airtight container and refrigerate until required.

TO SERVE

Smoked salmon balls, as above
1 tablespoon olive oil
60 g (2 oz/about 2 bunches) chives, finely chopped

Remove the salmon balls from the fridge and brush with olive oil. — Roll the salmon balls in finely chopped chives and carefully place onto platters to serve.

CHEF'S TIP
You can have these made and ready to go in the refrigerator, but once rolled in chives, make sure they are kept in an airtight container or the smell of chives will permeate everything around them.

Tuna, avocado, caviar

FROM THE PANTRY
Lemon olive oil
(Basics, page 218)

Nothing could be more elegant and delicious than simply sliced raw tuna, especially when served with rich and creamy avocado and sea-salty caviar. Order the tuna from your fishmonger for the day before, and wrap it in paper towel and plastic wrap overnight to help draw out excess moisture.

DAY BEFORE
Purchase tuna, remove bloodlines and skin and refrigerate.

TUNA

1 kg (2 lb 3 oz) piece of yellowfin tuna (midcut from the loin), sashimi-grade

Place the tuna on a clean cutting board, skin side up. — Remove the skin and discard. — Cut out any bloodline and be sure the fish is clean of any scales. — Wrap in paper towel and then wrap tightly in plastic wrap, and refrigerate for at least 6 hours. — Place on a cutting board and cut into 3 evenly sized blocks. — Slice each block into thin strips, and lay the strips on a tray lined with baking paper. Continue slicing the remaining tuna, covering each layer with baking paper, then refrigerate.

TO SERVE

2 avocados

sliced tuna, as above

100 ml (3½ fl oz) Lemon olive oil (Basics, page 218)

2 tablespoons white soy sauce

salt and cracked black pepper

Aleppo chilli flakes

50 g (1¾ oz) Oscietra caviar

Slice the avocados in half lengthways, and twist to separate the two halves. Remove the stone and carefully remove the skin. — Slice the avocados lengthways into long strips. — Place alternate layers of the avocado and the tuna over a 30 cm (12 in) round serving plate to give a chequered effect. — Drizzle the avocado and tuna with lemon olive oil and white soy sauce. — Season well with salt, cracked black pepper and Aleppo chilli. — Add little dobs of caviar on top and serve immediately.

CHEF'S TIP
The coldest part of your refrigerator is down the bottom, at the back. It's the perfect place to keep tuna at the lowest temperature possible.

San Daniele, Corella pears, lemony pink peppercorn oil

Lemon olive oil
(Basics, page 218)

PREP AHEAD
Make pink peppercorn oil.
Purchase Corella pears and
leave to ripen.

ON THE DAY
Slice Corella pears and
refrigerate.
Prep San Daniele 1 hour
before guests arrive.

This is a twist on the old classic of Parma ham and melon, replacing the melon with pears. It uses the same lemon olive oil from the tuna dish, but here it's infused with fruity, spicy pink peppercorns that complement both the San Daniele and the fruit. Don't forget to add a touch of salt to the pears, which lifts the flavour perceptibly.

LEMONY PINK PEPPERCORN OIL

20 g (¾ oz) pink peppercorns

90 ml (3 fl oz) Lemon olive oil
(Basics, page 218)

Heat a heavy cast-iron skillet or frying pan over a medium heat, then add the pink peppercorns. — Toast the peppercorns gently until fragrant, then remove from the heat. — Tip into a mortar and crush lightly with the pestle. — Combine the crushed peppercorns and lemon olive oil in a small saucepan and gently warm over low heat to infuse. Remove and set aside to cool.

CORELLA PEARS

2 ripe Corella pears

Cut the Corella pears in half and remove the core. — Cut each half into three even slices, giving a total of 12 wedges. — Refrigerate in an airtight container until required.

TO SERVE

6 paper-thin slices
San Daniele prosciutto

sliced Corella pears, as above

sea salt and freshly milled
black pepper

Pink peppercorn oil, as above

Arrange the San Daniele slices on two trays, separated from each other, then cover with a sheet of baking paper. — Leave at room temperature for an hour prior to serving. — Place the pear slices skin-side down on a tray and very lightly season with salt and pepper. — Tear each slice of San Daniele in half and drape half a slice over each pear slice. — Arrange on a serving platter and drizzle with the pink peppercorn oil. Serve immediately.

CHEF'S TIP
Instead of pears, use white
nectarines, peaches or apricots
when in season. Even persimmons
would complement the San Daniele,
and they would look amazing.

Crab, devilled egg, green toasts

FROM THE PANTRY
Seasoned rice-wine vinegar
(Basics, page 224)

DAY BEFORE

Pick herbs and store.

Make devilled egg mayonnaise.

Make mascarpone cream.

ON THE DAY

Bake baguette slices for
herb toast.

Chop herbs.

Cook crabmeat.

Some of you may remember the devilled egg, a cult dish popular during the 1970s as an appetiser or canapé for parties. Made with boiled eggs, the egg yolks are combined with mustard, creating a rich mayonnaise, which is then piped back into the boiled egg whites and dusted with paprika. That might raise a few eyebrows these days, so I've taken the best bit – the enriched egg yolk – and made it into a sauce to serve with fresh crab and little herb toasts, for an unforgettable start to the meal.

DEVILLED EGG MAYONNAISE

6 large eggs	
60 g (2 oz) mayonnaise (Kewpie/QP or whole egg)	
1 tablespoon Dijon mustard	
1 teaspoon chardonnay vinegar	
sea salt and pepper	
½ teaspoon smoked hot paprika	

MAKES 170 G (6 OZ)

Fill a 4 litre (135 fl oz) saucepan three-quarters full with cold water. — Add in the eggs, then bring to the boil and simmer for 7 minutes. Make an ice water bath by adding ice cubes to a bowl of cold water. — Remove the eggs using a slotted spoon and put them in the iced water. — Allow the eggs to completely cool before peeling. — Once peeled, pat the eggs dry on paper towel and slice them in half, removing the egg yolks. — (Reserve the cooked egg white for another dish. — Combine the egg yolks, mayonnaise, mustard, vinegar, sea salt, pepper and paprika in a food processor and blitz until smooth and creamy. — Check for seasoning, then refrigerate in an airtight container.

BAGUETTE TOASTS

1 day-old baguette	
60 ml (2 fl oz) olive oil	

Heat the oven to 170°C (340°F). — Slice the baguette on an angle, using a serrated knife, so that each slice is 20 cm (8 in) long but only ½ cm (¼ in) thick. You'll need 6 slices, but do a couple extra as backup. — Place the baguette slices on a heavy-duty baking tray lined with baking paper. — Brush both sides of each slice with olive oil and season with salt and pepper. — Place another sheet of baking paper on top, weighted down with a second tray. — Bake in the oven for around 8–10 minutes, until golden. — Remove the top baking tray and bake for a further 6–8 minutes, until the bread is crisp, then transfer to a wire rack until required.

MASCARPONE CREAM

100 g (3½ oz) mascarpone cheese	
60 g (2 oz) crème fraîche or sour cream	
1 tablespoon Dijon mustard	
30 g (1 oz/about ½ bunch) tarragon, leaves picked	
30 g (1 oz/½ bunch) dill, leaves picked	
30 g (1 oz/½ bunch) parsley, leaves picked	
1 bunch (30 g/1 oz) chives	

In a bowl, mix together the mascarpone cheese, crème fraîche and mustard. — Spoon the mixture into a plastic container with a lid, or into a piping (pastry) bag and tie off the end, then refrigerate until required. — Finely chop the herbs, then toss to combine. Refrigerate in an airtight container until required.

SPANNER CRAB

350 g (12½ oz) spanner crabmeat, raw	
100 g (3½ oz) unsalted butter	
sea salt and pepper	
1 tablespoon Seasoned rice-wine vinegar (Basics, page 224)	
1 teaspoon walnut oil (e.g. LeBlanc)	

Put the raw spanner crabmeat into a sieve set over a bowl. Cover with plastic wrap and refrigerate for 2 hours to allow excess water to drain. — Transfer the crabmeat to a tray and inspect it carefully, picking out any shell and discarding. — Refrigerate in an airtight container until required. — To cook, place a heavy-based saucepan over a medium heat and add the butter. — As soon as the butter melts and starts to bubble, add the crabmeat and cook gently, moving it with a spatula and taking care not to break up the chunks of meat. — Season well with salt and pepper, then transfer to a sieve set over a bowl. Allow the crabmeat to drain, then put it in a bowl and dress with the seasoned rice-wine vinegar, walnut oil, sea salt and pepper. — Set aside and keep warm.

CHEF'S TIP

You can buy pre-cooked crabmeat, but only buy the white meat for this dish. Drain and place into a container lined with paper towel. When ready to serve, warm through in a frying pan in melted butter and drain.

TO SERVE

6 Baguette toasts, page 194

Mascarpone cream, page 194

chopped, mixed herbs, page 194

Devilled egg mayonnaise, page 194

crabmeat, page 194

1 teaspoon smoked sweet paprika

Lay the toasted baguette slices out on a tray and spread or pipe the mascarpone cream on top. — Using a palette knife, spread the mixture to coat the entire surface of each toast. — Sprinkle with the chopped herbs, coating the entire surface. — Arrange six serving bowls on the bench and place a good spoonful of devilled egg mayonnaise on the base of each. — Spoon the warm crabmeat over the top, to cover, then dust with paprika. — Place a herb toast on the side of each bowl and serve immediately.

Just a prime rib (okay, with truffle)

Rendered beef fat
(Basics, page 222)

Mushroom stock
(Basics, page 220)

PREP AHEAD

Make spice mix and store
in an airtight container.

Purchase beef.

Render beef fat, if using.

DAY BEFORE

Unwrap beef rib and leave to air-
dry on a rack in the refrigerator.

ON THE DAY

Bring beef to room temperature.

Cook beef.

Make sauce.

CHEF'S TIP

If the beef is not dry-aged, it will
have more moisture, and the
rules change a little. Purchase
the rib up to 3 days before you
intend to cook it. Remove it
from any packaging and wipe
with paper towel, then wrap in
fresh paper towel and place on
a rack in the refrigerator, with
a rack beneath it, for around
6–12 hours. Then, remove the
paper and return the meat to
the rack in the refrigerator for
at least another 24 hours prior
to cooking. This will help dry
the outside of the meat and
concentrate its flavour.

There's nothing quite like the impact of a beautiful prime rib of dry-aged beef, slow-roasted at a low temperature. And as an added bonus, it gives you time to prepare everything else while it is cooking.

It's almost impossible to overcook, but do use a meat thermometer to keep an eye on the internal temperature of the meat. And if you are going to shave truffle all over it, make sure you do this at the table; the combined smells are nothing short of intoxicating.

SPICE MIX

1 tablespoon black peppercorns

1 tablespoon coriander seeds

1 teaspoon cumin seeds

1 teaspoon garlic powder

1 teaspoon onion powder

1 teaspoon soft dark brown sugar

1 tablespoon sweet
smoked paprika

1 teaspoon Aleppo chilli flakes

Combine the peppercorns, coriander seeds and cumin seeds in a frying pan and toast over a low–medium heat until fragrant. — Tip into a mortar and grind with a pestle until the mixture forms a fine powder. — Add the remaining ingredients and mix well together. — Store in an airtight container until required.

RIB OF BEEF

1.2 kg (2 lb 10 oz) rib of beef,
grain-fed, dry-aged

50 ml (1¾ fl oz) olive oil or
Rendered beef fat (Basics,
page 222)

2 red onions, cut into thick slices

½ bunch thyme

30 g (1 oz) spice mix, as above

40 g (1½ oz) fresh black
truffle, optional

Remove the rib from the refrigerator 2 hours prior to cooking, to come to room temperature. — Heat the oven to 85°C (185°F). — Turn the barbecue on to full, leaving the lid down so that it gets extremely hot. — Add half the olive oil or beef fat to the base of a roasting tray, then add the onions and thyme. Set aside. — Tie the beef rib tightly with butcher's twine to help it hold its shape while cooking. — Rub the beef rib all over with the remaining olive oil or beef fat, and season well with the spice mix. — Place onto the searing-hot barbecue and grill for 3–4 minutes on each side. — Turn the fat side to the heat and sear this as well. — Arrange the beef on the prepared roasting tray and bake in the oven until the internal temperature of the rib is at 58°C (135°F), about 3 hours. — Remove and keep in a warm place, lightly covered with aluminium foil. Rest the beef for at least 1 hour. You can hold it in a warm oven (50°C/120°F) for an hour or two before serving. — Drain the pan juices, along with the onions, and set aside in a small pan.

TRUFFLE SAUCE

100 ml (3½ fl oz) pan juices and
onions, as above

150 ml (5 fl oz) Mushroom stock
(Basics, page 220)

1 tablespoon red-wine vinegar,
e.g. Forvm cabernet sauvignon

1 teaspoon freshly chopped
truffle or truffle paste

2–3 tablespoons butter

In a small, heavy-based saucepan, combine the pan juices and onions, mushroom stock and vinegar and simmer until the volume is reduced by half. — Strain through a sieve into a clean saucepan, squeezing out as much liquid as possible. — Using a hand-held blender, blitz in the truffle and butter. Season as required, and keep warm. You can do this around 2 hours prior if you like.

TO SERVE

Rib of beef, as above

Truffle sauce, as above

sea salt

fresh truffle, optional

Place the beef on a cutting board and remove the rib bone by slicing down between the bone and the meat. — Cut the meat into 1 cm (½ in) thick slices, across the grain, and reassemble on a warmed serving plate with a lip. — Brush with a little of the sauce and season with sea salt. — Serve with the truffle sauce, placing the bone on the side. — If using fresh truffle, shave it finely and generously over the beef to completely cover it.

Straw potatoes, truffle salt

Prep potatoes and fry
up to 3 hours prior.

These are, quite simply, next-level French fries, the traditional *pommes paille* of France, high on impact and crunch. Unlike regular fries, which need to be cooked twice or even three times, these are only fried once – and you can keep them warm in the oven until ready to serve.

Season well with truffle salt immediately after frying for that extra deliciousness that makes them so moreish. Just leave some for the guests.

STRAW POTATOES

1 kg (2 lb 3 oz) desiree, russet or sebago potatoes	
2 litres (68 fl oz) vegetable oil	
truffle salt	

CHEF'S TIP
Make sure that the potatoes are as dry as possible before frying, otherwise the moisture in the potato will cause the oil to expand and overflow. For this reason, it's a good idea to fry in small batches, and just take your time.

Peel the potatoes and rinse under cold water. — Using a mandoline, cut the potatoes into matchsticks around 6–7 cm (2½–2¾ in) long. — Rinse under cold running water until the water runs clear and the starch is washed from the potatoes. — Drain well and pat dry with paper towel. Spread the matchsticks out on a dry cloth to get extra moisture out of them. — To fry, heat the vegetable oil in an 8 litre (270 fl oz) heavy-based pot to 190°C (375°F). — Fry the potatoes in very small batches – I suggest just a handful at a time – and be careful, as the oil will rise up and could overflow. — Stir occasionally until the potatoes turn golden and create no more bubbles, then remove, shake well to remove excess oil, and place on a tray lined with paper towel. — Season well with the truffle salt, while still hot. — Repeat until all the potato straws are cooked. — Serve at room temperature or keep in a warm (50°C/120°F) oven until ready to serve. — Pile high in a warm bowl to serve.

Watercress salad, go-to honey mustard dressing

Make the dressing and refrigerate in an airtight jar.

Wash and dry the salad leaves and refrigerate in an airtight container.

This light and simple salad will add freshness to any dinner party. This dressing is my go-to when I want to add a light sweetness to mixed leaves, rocket, baby spinach, mizuna or cos (romaine). This recipe makes 210 ml (7 fl oz) of honey mustard dressing, enough for about three salads.

GO-TO HONEY MUSTARD DRESSING

60 ml (2 fl oz) red-wine vinegar, e.g. Forvm cabernet sauvignon	
1 teaspoon honey	
1 tablespoon shallot, finely diced	
freshly milled black pepper	
pinch of sea salt	
2 level tablespoons grain mustard	
120 ml (4 fl oz) olive oil	

ON THE DAY
Shake the dressing to bring it together, and dress the salad.

In a small pan, combine the red-wine vinegar and honey, and bring to a boil. — Remove from the heat and add the diced shallot, black pepper and salt, whisking to combine. — Set aside to cool completely. — Once cool, whisk in the grain mustard and then the olive oil until emulsified, and set aside. — If making ahead, whisk or shake the dressing just before serving, to emulsify the oil and vinegar.

TO SERVE

150 g (5½ oz) watercress, or your choice of leaves	
60 g (2 oz) Go-to honey mustard dressing, as above	

CHEF'S TIP
This honey mustard dressing can be used in any salad – it's a fabulous go-to, hence the name!

Put the leaves into a large mixing bowl and drizzle with the dressing. — Using your hands, toss the leaves in the dressing, then transfer to a serving bowl, and serve.

THE DINNER PARTY

Bitter chocolate tart, Pedro Ximénez dates

PREP AHEAD
Cook dates a week in advance.

This bitter chocolate tart is based on the classic tarte au chocolat amer, of the late French chef Joel Robuchon. I remember making it so many times when it was *the* go-to restaurant dessert about 30 years ago, so it has certainly stood the test of time. (Of course it has, it's incredible.) I've added a little twist here, with a fine layer of dates cooked in rich, raisiny Pedro Ximénez sherry – so fudgy and decadent. Serve with the Mascarpone cream (page 38) for even more decadence.

DAY BEFORE

Make tart base and store.

Make Mascarpone cream (page 36).

ON THE DAY

Bake tart and leave to cool. Do not refrigerate!

Make chocolate cream in the morning.

Allow tart to set for 5 hours before cutting.

CHOCOLATE TART BASE

60 g (2 oz) egg yolks
200 g (7 oz) unsalted butter, softened
80 g (2¾ oz) caster (superfine) sugar
200 g (7 oz) plain (all-purpose) flour, plus extra for dusting
3 level tablespoons cocoa powder
pinch of salt

Whisk the egg yolks in a small bowl. — Using a stand mixer with a paddle attachment, beat the butter and sugar on high speed until light and pale. — Drop the speed to medium, then add the egg yolks slowly, beating to combine. — Sift together the plain flour, cocoa powder and salt, then add to the bowl while mixing on low–medium speed until it just comes together – do not overwork. — Remove from the bowl and knead quickly together until smooth. — Wrap the pastry in plastic wrap and flatten out into a disc. — Refrigerate for at least 1 hour before use. — When ready to bake, heat the oven to 165°C (330°F). — Spray a 22 cm (8¾ in) tart ring with a removable base with baker's spray. — Remove the pastry from the refrigerator and remove the plastic wrap. — Lightly dust the benchtop with flour, then knead the pastry in the flour to soften. — Using a rolling pin, roll out the pastry to around 7 mm (¼ in) thick. The pastry is very soft and will break; it's okay, just push it back together. — Continue rolling the pastry until you have a disc around 25 cm (10 in) wide – larger than the tart base. — Place the tart base on top of the pastry and then use a knife to cut around the base. Discard the trimmings. — Gently push the tart base under the disc of pastry, then drop it back into the tart case. — Using your fingers, press the pastry against the sides of the tart case so that the base is completely sealed with the pastry. — Lightly prick the pastry all over with a fork, then freeze the tart case for 30 minutes prior to baking. — Bake the tart for around 30 minutes, or until the base is slightly firm to the touch – it will firm up more as it cools. — Remove from the oven and allow to cool on a rack. — Store in an airtight container until required.

PEDRO XIMÉNEZ DATES

200 ml (7 fl oz) Pedro Ximénez sherry
250 g (9 oz) medjool dates, pitted

Pour the Pedro Ximénez into a saucepan and reduce by half, being careful not to flame the alcohol. — Chop the dates and add to the reduction. — Simmer gently until you have a thick, sweet paste. — Remove from the heat and set aside to cool to room temperature. — Cut two sheets of baking paper into about 25 cm (10 in) squares and lightly spray one side of each with baker's spray. — Lightly dampen your hands and roll the date paste into a ball. — Press the ball into the centre of the baking paper, then place the second sheet of baking paper on top. — Using a rolling pin, roll the ball out to around 20 cm (8 in) in diameter. — Remove the top sheet of baking paper, peel the date puree off the bottom sheet, and put it in the blind-baked tart base, leaving a 1 cm (½ in) border between the edge of the tart base and the date, so the chocolate will cover the date puree completely when poured on top.

TO FILL AND BAKE THE TART

240 g (8½ oz) dark chocolate, chopped (Valrhona Manjari 64%)	
1 large egg	
1 egg yolk	
240 g (8½ oz) thickened (whipping) cream	
70 ml (2¼ fl oz) full-cream milk	
pinch of salt	

CHEF'S TIP

This tart has pastry on the bottom only, but not the sides. I find this is simpler to do, and it looks great.

Heat the oven to 110°C (230°F). — Put the chocolate in a large, heatproof bowl and set to one side. — Whisk the egg and the egg yolk in a separate bowl until completely smooth, then strain through a small sieve and set to one side. — Pour the cream, milk and salt into a medium, heavy-based pot and bring to the boil. — Once boiling, pour the mixture over the chocolate and, using a spatula, stir until the chocolate is completely melted and smooth. — Add the whisked egg to the chocolate mixture and stir well until the chocolate cream is incorporated and the mixture looks rich, smooth and shiny. — Pour the mixture onto the prepared base, and bake for 10 minutes. Be brave – the chocolate should still wobble when shaken. — Remove and keep at room temperature (do not refrigerate) for at least 4–5 hours prior to serving. — To serve, cut into slices at the table, and pass around a bowl of mascarpone cream.

CHICKEN –
A LIFE LESSON

When people come to dinner at the home of a three-hat chef, they come with expectations. Will there be caviar, wagyu beef and lobster? Ancient wine and contemporary cocktails? Will it be like a fine-dining restaurant?

Potentially, yes. But sometimes, I just roast a chicken.

He roasted a chicken??? They don't say it out loud, but I can tell they are dismayed by what they think is a simple meal that anyone could make.

But, as they say in that cult classic Australian film, *The Castle*, 'It's what you do with it.'

The trick is in making something simple, special.

I don't just roast a chicken.

I. Roast. A. Chicken.

And that starts with the chicken that you bring home.

BUYING CHICKEN

I am not going to harp on about buying organic or free-range chickens over factory farmed. If you care enough about good food to be reading this book, then you know that you get what you pay for when it comes to chicken.

By buying better quality, you're also supporting those who are embracing sustainable farming techniques and using more humane systems that allow the birds to live in an environment where they can grow naturally, foraging and roaming freely. This results not only in a more ethical purchase, but a better one, too.

Because the chicken has been allowed to roam, there is a more even fat distribution and muscle structure that develops flavour, and when cooked, it will lose less moisture through shrinkage.

With farming chicken, as with cooking chicken, it's what you do with it.

Look for organic or free-range birds from your local butcher, who in turn supports sustainable and regenerative farmers.

A tip: Try to purchase chickens that are packed in tight-fitting bags; air around the bird is its enemy.

Another tip: Check the process date or the best-before date – it should be at least eight days away, so you know it will be at its best.

One of the best lessons you can learn is to buy whole birds and break them down (joint them) yourself. It's a very simple skill to learn, but makes all the difference to the quality.

Purchasing cut chicken pieces means the chicken has already been handled, possibly by several people. There is no way of knowing how fresh it is or how well it has been stored. Meat that has already been cut will deteriorate much faster than a whole, freshly packed chicken.

STORING CHICKEN

As soon as you open the door of your refrigerator, warm air rushes in and pushes the cold air out. We also know that hot air rises, which means the cold air holds in the bottom of the refrigerator, causing less fluctuation of temperature to the bird itself.

So store the chickens on a tray in the coldest part of your refrigerator: on the bottom shelf, at the very back.

If you store the chicken at the top of the refrigerator, it could be a degree or two warmer, which will diminish the quality and freshness, perhaps by days. It also increases the possibility of spillage or contamination, neither of which are ideal.

IT'S WHAT YOU DO WITH IT

I know I keep saying this, but it could not be truer. When buying chickens I purchase several birds which I break down as I need. The crown of the chicken – the breast on the bone – could be roasted, or I might remove the breasts and pan fry them.

I save the legs and thighs (Marylands), and the wings, separately and freeze them. That way I can save up enough thighs for a curry, or enough wings for BBQ spicy wings.

That leaves me the other bones and carcass, which I also freeze for a future chicken stock (Basics, page 215).

There are so many delicious ways to eat chicken. Check out the braised chicken thighs in the 'Family Knows Best' menu (page 114) – the thighs for this dish can be saved up and frozen prior, and then simply defrosted and braised.

Then there's the Blackened piri-piri chicken from the 'Variety is The Spice of Life' menu (page 135), where the chicken is brined and butterflied, then marinated in chilli paste prior to roasting in a hot oven to blacken the skin.

There is so much more to the humble chicken, whether it's a no-brainer weekday dinner, a cracking dinner party dish, or the next-level roast chicken I've shared here.

It really is what you do with it.

Next-level roast chicken

FROM THE PANTRY
Best-ever brine
(Basics, page 214)

DAY BEFORE

Brine chicken for
12 hours overnight.

Make stuffing and
refrigerate.

ON THE DAY

Stuff chicken and leave
uncovered on a rack in
the refrigerator.

Remove 30 minutes
before roasting.

Brined overnight, stuffed and roasted with butter, this dish will fulfil all your roast chicken dreams.

The traditional way to stuff a chicken is to fill the cavity of the bird before roasting, but it takes a long time for the heat to reach the inside of the stuffing, resulting in dry, overcooked meat. The best and most effective way is to stuff the bird between the breast and the skin. This helps protect the breast meat from over-cooking, while at the same time virtually basting the meat, thanks to the butter in the stuffing.

Given that the legs always take longer to cook, this is the best way of protecting the breast meat.

Another good tip: Cook the bird and then leave it to rest for 1–2 hours before serving; it really makes a difference.

FOR THE BRINING

1.6 kg (3½ lb) chicken, organic, free range

1 batch Best-ever brine
(Basics, page 214)

Rinse the chicken under cold water and remove any innards from the cavity. — Using a paring knife, remove the wishbone by scraping along the side of the bone on each side. — Use your fingers to find the top of the bone, then pinch and twist it to pull it out. — Pat dry with paper towel. — Pour the brine into a large enough container to hold both brine and chicken. — Submerge the chicken completely in the brine, then cover with a lid and refrigerate for 12 hours. — Drain well, discarding the brine, and pat the chicken dry with paper towel. — Place on a rack set above a tray, ready to be stuffed.

FOR THE STUFFING

250 g (9 oz) unsalted butter, softened

55 g (2 oz) fresh brioche crumbs or fresh breadcrumbs

sea salt and pepper

1 tablespoon parsley, chopped

Mix all the ingredients together in a bowl until well combined and smooth. — Scrape all the stuffing mix into a piping (pastry) bag, and tie off the end. — Hold at room temperature if you are going to stuff the bird on the same day, otherwise refrigerate, and take it out of the fridge a few hours before you intend to use the stuffing. — Use your fingers to loosen the skin away from the breast meat. Starting at the top of the crown with the legs facing you, push your fingers under the skin from the pointy end of the breast, and run your fingers gently between the skin and the flesh, until you can reach all the way across. — Cut the tip off the piping bag and push it into the bird under the skin, piping in all the stuffing. — Use your hands to push and spread the stuffing evenly across the breast. — Truss the chicken with kitchen twine to keep the legs and wings tucked in close to the body. — Place on a rack over a tray, and refrigerate for at least 4 hours before roasting, so that the skin can dry before cooking.

TO ROAST THE CHICKEN

50 g (1¾ oz) unsalted butter, softened

sea salt, pepper

Heat the oven to 220°C (430°F). — Remove the chicken from the refrigerator and leave at room temperature for around 30 minutes. — Brush the chicken all over with the soft butter, making sure it is evenly covered. — Season with salt and pepper. — Pour a cup full of cold water and a drizzle of olive oil into the bottom of a roasting tin, then add the chicken. — Roast for around 50 minutes, turning the tray around in the oven halfway through. — Remove from the oven and hold in a warm place to rest for at least 60 minutes. Reserve the pan juices. — Rest in a warm place for 30 minutes, then lightly cover the chicken with foil.

CHEF'S TIP

Be sure to discard the brine
after use.

CHEF'S TIP

It's a good idea to roast the chicken so that it comes out of the oven just before your guests arrive. Not only will the aromas be wonderful, but resting it for a couple of hours in a warm place will keep the chicken succulent. Do not cover the bird when it first comes out of the oven, or the skin will no longer be crisp – allow to cool for at least 30 minutes before lightly covering with foil.

TO SERVE

chicken (page 205), roasted and rested

buttery pan juices from the roasting tin

Set the chicken aside on a chopping board. — Scrape the buttery pan juices from the roasting dish into a small saucepan. — Bring to a boil and whisk to combine, then remove from the heat. — Strain into a serving jug and keep warm. — Carve the chicken by first removing the trussing string. — Remove each leg and separate the thigh from the drumstick, then cut each thigh in half and place on a serving platter. — Remove the wings and place with the legs. — Remove the breasts from the crown carefully, so as not to loosen the stuffing, then cut each breast into 5 pieces, and place on the serving platter. — Turn the bird over and cut out the chicken oysters, and arrange on the serving platter with the rest of the chicken. — Serve with the warm pan juices.

THE COCKTAILS

MARTINEZ
WHISKY SOUR
CLASSIC NEGRONI
HANKY PANKY
GIMLET
SUNSET LILLET ROSÉ
THE LAST WORD
MANHATTAN
THE DRY MARTINI

The perfect dinner party needs just the right cocktail to start the evening with an elegant bang. Here are some of our favourite tipples matched to each occasion. Each recipe makes one drink – but of course, you can make as many as you like!

Martinez

The Martinez is often referred to as the precursor to the Martini. The original is made with an Old Tom gin, which is a little sweeter but, made with dry gin, it becomes even more special.

45 ml (1½ fl oz) dry gin
45 ml (1½ fl oz) Carpano Antica Formula vermouth
10 ml (¼ fl oz) Luxardo maraschino liqueur
2 dashes Angostura bitters
one strip lemon rind, no white pith

Combine all the ingredients, except the lemon rind, in a mixing glass. — Stir with ice for about 30 seconds, then strain into a chilled cocktail glass. — Squeeze the lemon rind over the cocktail to express the oils. — Twist the lemon rind into a spiral, add to the cocktail and serve.

Whisky Sour

The first mention of the Whisky Sour was in 1862, in *The Bartenders Guide* by Jerry Thomas.

Travelling by sea was particularly difficult in the 1800s, as was access to clean, fresh water on long voyages, making whisky, rum and other spirits very popular with sailors. Many sailors suffered from of a lack of vitamin C, so they would take huge amounts of lemons and limes on these voyages to combat disease.

Of course, they would also bring alcohol, such as whisky and bourbon.

The classic recipe for a Whisky Sour is so simple: whisky, lemon and simple syrup. The drink needs only three ingredients to be delicious.

Nowadays, many bartenders like to add egg white to create that foamy texture, but I prefer the crisp version.

45 ml (1½ fl oz) Hibiki Japanese whisky
25 ml (¾ fl oz) lemon juice
15 ml (½ fl oz) Simple syrup (see below)
3 dashes Angostura bitters
1 maraschino cherry, for garnish (optional)

Combine all the liquid ingredients in a chilled mixing glass. — Add ice and shake vigorously for about 45 seconds. — Strain into a chilled rocks glass or highball glass. — Garnish with a maraschino cherry if you want to fancy it up!

SIMPLE SYRUP

250 ml (8½ fl oz/1 cup) water, preferably filtered
220 g (8 oz/1 cup) granulated sugar

Heat the water in a small saucepan over a low–medium heat until hot, but don't bring to a full boil. — Add the sugar and stir constantly until fully dissolved. — Let the syrup cool to room temperature before using or storing. — Pour the simple syrup into a glass jar and store in the refrigerator for up to 4 weeks.

Classic Negroni

This classic was created for Count Camillo Negroni in 1919 at Florence's Café Casoni. Apparently, the Count demanded that the bartender strengthen his favourite cocktail, the Americano, by replacing the soda water (club soda) with gin. The bartender garnished the drink with an orange peel rather than the traditional lemon peel, and the Negroni was born.

30 ml (1 fl oz) gin
30 ml (1 fl oz) Campari
30 ml (1 fl oz) Carpano Antica Formula vermouth
1 slice of orange peel, for garnish

Add the gin, Campari and vermouth to a mixing glass filled with ice, and stir until well-chilled. — Strain into a rocks glass filled with large ice cubes. — Garnish with the orange peel.

Hanky Panky

The Hanky Panky was invented by the one and only ever female head bartender at the Savoy Hotel in London. Ada Coleman created this classic in the early 1900s for a famous actor, Sir Charles Hawtrey, who called it 'the real hanky panky'. We're big fans of a little hanky panky – the cocktail, of course.

45 ml (1½ fl oz) gin
45 ml (1½ fl oz) Carpano Antica Formula vermouth
2 dashes Fernet-Branca
1 slice of orange peel, for garnish

Combine the gin, vermouth and Fernet-Branca in a mixing glass filled with ice. — Stir well for at least 30 seconds, then strain into a chilled cocktail glass. — Twist the orange peel over the drink to express its oils, then use it as a garnish.

Gimlet

The Gimlet is a classic gin-based cocktail that was created in the mid-1800s. It was supposedly named for naval medical officer Thomas Desmond Gimlette, who devised it as a way of getting sailors to drink lime juice to prevent scurvy while away at sea. Some recipes call for lime cordial, but we prefer icy cold fresh lime juice.

60 ml (2 fl oz) gin
30 ml (1 fl oz) fresh lime juice
20 ml (¾ fl oz) Simple syrup (see page 210)
1 slice of lime, for garnish

Combine gin, lime juice and simple syrup in a cocktail shaker filled with ice. — Shake vigorously, then strain into a chilled coupe glass. — Garnish with a slice of lime.

Sunset Lillet Rosé

A wine-based aperitif from Bordeaux, Lillet Rosé is all berries and blossoms, with a hint of grapefruit; the perfect drink to end the day and begin the night.

Alternatively, pour 60 ml (2 fl oz) Lillet Rosé into a glass filled with ice and top up with tonic water.

60 ml (2 fl oz) Lillet Rosé
60 ml (2 fl oz) fresh grapefruit juice
30 ml (1 fl oz) gin
1 slice of grapefruit (for garnish), optional

Combine Lillet Rosé, grapefruit juice and gin in a cocktail shaker filled with ice. — Shake vigorously. — Strain and pour into a chilled cocktail glass. — Garnish with a slice of grapefruit if you like (I prefer not to!). — Serve immediately.

The Last Word

I was at the now-closed Pegu Club in New York, and absolutely everyone was drinking this pale mint green drink with a red cherry. So New York! The Last Word is a unique and classic chartreuse cocktail whose equal parts work in perfect harmony, beautifully balanced between sharp, sour and sweet. It sounds wrong, but it's oh so right. And that's the last word on The Last Word.

30 ml (1 fl oz) gin
30 ml (1 fl oz) green Chartreuse liqueur
30 ml (1 fl oz) Luxardo maraschino liqueur
30 ml (1 fl oz) fresh lime juice
1 cherry for garnish, (optional; if in season)

Combine the gin, Chartreuse, maraschino liqueur and lime juice in a cocktail shaker. — Fill with ice and shake vigorously. — Strain into a coupe glass. — Garnish with a fresh cherry, if using.

Manhattan

The origins of this cocktail date back to the 1860s, but the details are rather murky. The most common theory is that it was created at the Manhattan Club in New York, as a signature cocktail for a dinner hosted by Winston Churchill's mother. Turns out she was in Europe at the time, having just given birth to Winston, but never let the truth get in the way of a good story.

60 ml (2 fl oz) rye whisky
30 ml (1 fl oz) Carpano Antica Formula vermouth
2 dashes Angostura bitters

Add the rye whisky, vermouth and bitters to a mixing glass with ice, and stir until well chilled. — Strain into a chilled coupe glass. — No garnish – less is more!

The Dry Martini

Always, always stirred. So much more elegant than shaking, stirring creates a strong and velvety smooth texture, whereas shaking adds tiny particles of ice that dilute the martini and make it cloudy. A martini needs clarity!

15 ml (½ fl oz) dry vermouth, e.g. Noilly Prat
60 ml (2 fl oz) London dry gin
olives or a twist of lemon, for garnish

Fill a metal cocktail shaker with cracked ice. — Pour in the dry vermouth, stir briefly, then strain into a jug. — Add the gin and stir briskly for about 10 seconds. — Strain into a chilled cocktail glass, and garnish with olives or a twist of lemon – whatever you like!

THE BASICS

These recipes will be your best friends, either in preparation for entertaining, or to utilise on a daily basis for weekday meals.

There's little point in making a tiny amount of flavoured oil, for instance, for just one dinner party. Besides, it's really hard to get the depth of flavour you want when making a small quantity. But make up a full batch beforehand, and it'll be there to spice up a midweek takeaway or add oomph to a casual weekend brunch.

Take chicken stock. I've written the recipe so that you can use a pot of around 6 litre (202 fl oz) capacity, which will give you around 2.5 litres (85 fl oz) of chicken stock to use and store in the freezer. But I also suggest you invest in a 12 litre (405 fl oz) pot, and double the recipe, thereby ensuring you have a constant supply. In a restaurant, these large amounts are like money in the bank; absolute building blocks of flavour.

Besides, chicken stock is a staple that you should always have ready to go. It's great to add to braises, sauces, curries, soups, or rice dishes, and because you made it yourself, you'll know exactly what went into it.

Nobody is going to make all these basic recipes in one go, but once you get used to having them in the pantry, you'll probably find yourself in a constant cycle of renewal. I get heart palpitations when I'm running low on my essential red sauce or shellfish oil, and start to panic if I think I could run out at any time. That's why I save prawn (shrimp) shells or over-ripe tomatoes as I go, and freeze them. It's such a good feeling knowing that you have the 'bones' to make the next thing you want, before you even need to make it.

And with food waste being such a big issue, the fact that you're using everything you can also feels good. All these items have a good shelf life, too, whether stored in the pantry, refrigerator or freezer.

As I said, think of them as your best friends. They'll be there when you need them, every time.

Benno's hot miso mustard

MAKES 360 G (12½ OZ)

It was way back in the dawn of my restaurant Sepia that I came up with the idea to mix the condiment of my heritage – hot English mustard – with that of the smooth, slightly sweet, saikyo miso paste (shiro miso), made from rice. This umami hit is magnificent with any cooked meat, and can be prepared well in advance and kept in the refrigerator. And don't save it for special occasions! A spoonful of Benno's hot miso mustard turns the simplest steak or salmon dish into a special occasion in its own right.

1 lemon
300 g (10½ oz) saikyo miso (white miso)
60 g (2 oz) hot English mustard (e.g. Tracklements)

Zest and juice the lemon, then strain the juice back over the zest. — Mix the miso paste and hot English mustard together in a bowl. — Add the lemon juice and zest, and stir until smooth. — Refrigerate in an airtight container for up to 1 month. — Use with everything.

Best-ever brine

MAKES 4.3 LITRES (145 FL OZ)

It's time to brine! This little chef's secret is out: a well-brined piece of meat will rock your world. If you have not brined chicken for a roast dinner yet, you haven't lived.

Soaking the meat in salted water, which is essentially what brining is, will keep it incredibly moist, as well as imparting more flavour and seasoning, without it actually tasting salty.

You can make this recipe your own by adding different flavours, so long as you don't change the salinity of the brine or the length of time. The proportion of salt should be anywhere between 4–8 per cent of the water volume. Be sure to discard the brine after use, as it's unsafe to use it again.

300 g (10½ oz) table salt (7.5%)
100 g (3½ oz) soft brown sugar (2.5%)
60 ml (2 fl oz) dark soy sauce (1.5%)
100 ml (3½ fl oz) mirin (2.5%)
1 tablespoon black peppercorns
1 teaspoon fennel seeds
zest of 1 lemon
3 bay leaves
30 g (1 oz/about ½ bunch) thyme, whole sprigs
2 garlic cloves

Pour 1 litre (34 fl oz) of water into a heavy-based pot and bring to the boil. — Add the remaining ingredients. — Bring back to the boil and simmer for 1–2 minutes, until the salts and sugars have dissolved and the spices and aromatics are fragrant. — Turn off the heat, then add the remaining 3 litres (101 fl oz) of water. Leave to cool. — Once cold, pour into a container large enough to hold the liquid as well as the chicken – about 6–7 litres (202–236 fl oz). — Refrigerate, and allow the brine to cool to 5°C (40°F). You're ready to go forth and brine.

CHEF'S TIP

The brine has to be cold before you use it, but this recipe uses a handy shortcut: you infuse just 1 litre (34 fl oz) of water with the salt and aromatics, then cool it down with the remaining 3 litres (101 fl oz) of water. You can even add ice cubes to the second batch of water, if you're really short on time.

Chicken stock

MAKES 2 LITRES (68 FL OZ)

A great home-made chicken stock is a good friend to have. Keep it in the freezer, ready to call on for soups, broths, sauces, braises, curries and rice dishes. Making your own is one of the most rewarding things you can do in the kitchen, because it means you know exactly what went into it.

It can also save you money. If you reserve and freeze the chicken bones and carcass each time you break down (joint) the chickens, you'll soon have enough to make a sizeable amount of stock. (If you have a 12 litre/405 fl oz pot – and space in the freezer – then double the recipe.)

You'll notice that my recipe is quite simple and pure. Some cooks put a lot of vegetables in their chicken stock, but I find too many aromatics can overpower the chicken's sweet meatiness. You're better off keeping it neutral, and then you can adapt it to different recipes.

2.5 kg (5½ lb) chicken carcasses, excess fat removed
3.5 litres (118 fl oz) water
2 onions, cut into quarters
1 bay leaf
30 g (1 oz/about ½ bunch) thyme, whole sprigs
16 peppercorns

Put the chicken carcasses in a sink under cold running water. — Clean the fat from the bones and remove any internal organs from inside the carcasses. — Drain the carcasses, then put them in a 6–8 litre (202–270 fl oz) stockpot. — Fill the pot with enough cold water to cover the carcasses, then bring to the boil. — Skim off any impurities that rise to the surface, and reduce the heat to a gentle simmer. — For a very pure stock, repeat this process with fresh cold water, once again bringing the water to a simmer. — Simmer for an hour, skimming regularly and keeping the water topped up. — Add the onions, herbs and peppercorns and simmer for a further 90 minutes, until the stock smells aromatic. — Turn off the heat and leave to stand for 30 minutes. — Pass the stock through a fine strainer and cool in containers. — Once cold, refrigerate for up to 3 days, or freeze in batches.

Clarified butter

MAKES 1.2 KG (2 LB 10 OZ)

Clarified butter is the clear, golden butter fat left after removing the buttermilk and water. It's great to have on hand for frying fish and meat, because it has a high smoking point, which means it won't burn as quickly as regular butter. Use it for poaching, too – not only does it have great flavour, it also maintains a consistent temperature.

The easiest way to clarify butter is to let the oven do the work for you, melting the butter and allowing the milk solids to settle at the bottom. Then you can keep the pure golden butter in the refrigerator for up to 3 months, or freeze it.

2 kg (4 lb 6 oz) unsalted butter

Heat the oven to 100°C (210°F). — Put the butter in a heavy-based, ovenproof saucepan, cover, and heat in the oven for around 90 minutes. — Remove and skim away any foam on the surface. — Strain the golden fat from the butter through a paper coffee filter or muslin cloth (cheesecloth) into a container, removing the white liquid milk solids and reserving the golden liquid fat. — Refrigerate for 24 hours until set, then drain off any milk solids that may have gathered, and pat dry. — Store in the refrigerator for up to 3 months, or freeze.

Crispy rayu chilli

MAKES 450 G (1 LB)

Just a spoonful of this fiery, crispy, no-cook sesame chilli oil, and bang! You're transported to the streets of old Tokyo, a steamy bowl of ramen in front of you. This is a very real weapon in the artillery of the home pantry, and makes a dinner party (and possibly your friends, as well) sing. Use the leftovers to jazz up noodle dishes, barbecued meats and grilled fish, or just use it as a table condiment – with a legal disclaimer as to its heat, of course.

75 g (2¾ oz) fried shallots, store bought
2½ tablespoons (25 g/1 oz) fried garlic, store bought
1 teaspoon (10 g/¼ oz) dried shrimp, store bought and ground (optional)
1 tablespoon (10 g/¼ oz) toasted sesame seeds
50 g (1¾ oz) Korean hot chilli flakes (gochugaru)
1 teaspoon (5 g/⅛ oz) salt
1 teaspoon (5 g/⅛ oz) sugar
300 g (10½ oz) Fragrant chilli oil (Basics, page 216)

Combine fried shallots, garlic, ground dried shrimp, sesame seeds, chilli flakes salt and sugar in a bowl. — Toss until mixed, then drizzle over the chilli oil and toss well. — Seal in an airtight container at room temperature, until required.

Essential red sauce

MAKES 2.5 LITRES (85 FL OZ)

This magnificent tomato sugo is a life-saver, and one of my all-time must-haves in the freezer. As soon as I get down to my last container, I make more, ensuring there is never a gap in supply. That's why I call it essential: because it is super delicious, elegant with a punch, and can always be relied on to get you out of a tight situation.

It can multi-task from one end of the week to the other, forming the base of a simple pasta, enriching a braise, adding magic to a bolognese sauce, or spooned over steak, pizzaiola style. And don't get me started on how good it is in a chicken parmigiana.

60 ml (2 fl oz) olive oil
4 large brown onions, finely diced
6 garlic cloves, minced
1 bird's eye chilli, finely chopped (optional)
1 long red chilli, finely sliced and seeds removed
20 g (¾ oz/about ½ bunch) fresh thyme, leaves picked
1 × 60 g (2 oz) piece of smoked pancetta
2 teaspoons salt
1 teaspoon whole black peppercorns
420 g (15 oz) tomato paste (concentrated purée), e.g. Mutti
1 teaspoon hot smoked paprika
4 × 400 g (14 oz) tins of tomatoes, chopped, e.g. Mutti
700 g (1 lb 9 oz) fresh roma (plum) tomatoes, chopped
1 litre (34 fl oz) Chicken stock (Basics, page 215) or vegetable stock
2 tablespoons sugar

Heat a large, heavy-based saucepan over a medium–high heat. — Heat the olive oil, then add the chopped onions, garlic and chillies and cook, stirring, for 5 minutes. — Add the thyme, pancetta, salt and peppercorns and continue to cook over a medium heat for a further 5–10 minutes, until the onions start to soften and lightly caramelise. — Add the tomato paste and paprika and cook for a further 3–4 minutes. — Add the canned and fresh tomatoes, stock and sugar, and bring to a simmer, stirring. — Turn the heat to very low and simmer gently for 3 hours, until the sauce is thick and rich. — Remove the pancetta, then lightly whiz the sauce with a hand-held blender. — Return to a low heat and continue to reduce for a further 30–50 minutes, until thick and dark red. — Cool, then freeze in 1 litre (34 fl oz) batches.

CHEF'S TIP

For a vegetarian version, drop the pancetta and swap the chicken stock for vegetable stock.

Fragrant chilli oil

MAKES 1.25 LITRES (42 FL OZ)

I first learnt to make fragrant chilli oil when I was living in Hong Kong many years ago, and my recipe has changed and evolved ever since, as good recipes do. One of the most interesting developments has come from using different styles of chillies, to introduce smokiness and fruitiness as well as heat. Other good moves have included adding dried shrimps or dried scallops, black beans or sesame seeds. It's worth making a large quantity of this, so you can give some to friends as gifts.

100 g (3½ oz) Korean chilli flakes (gochugaru)
30 g (1 oz) Sichuan peppercorns
1 star anise, lightly crushed
2 fresh cayenne chillies, sliced, seeds retained
1 knob ginger (about 25 g/1 oz), thinly sliced
2 garlic cloves, thinly sliced
50 g (1¾ oz) dried chiles de árbol (small red chilli), chopped
50 g (1¾ oz) dried ancho chilli, chopped
50 g (1¾ oz) dried chipotle chilli, chopped
3 dried habanero chillies, chopped
1.3 litres (44 fl oz) roasted rapeseed oil (caiziyou) or grapeseed oil

In a large 6 litre (202 fl oz) casserole dish, mix the Korean chilli flakes, Sichuan pepper, star anise, fresh chilli, ginger, garlic and the dried chopped chillies until well combined. — Divide the oil equally between two heavy-based pans, heating one batch to 180°C (360°F) and the other batch to 130°C (265°F). — Put the casserole dish containing the chilli under the extraction hood on its highest setting. — Carefully pour the 180°C (360°F) oil over the chilli mixture in one go, allowing the chillies to bubble and seethe. — Once the chillies have stopped bubbling, pour the 130°C (265°F) oil over the top. — Leave the chillies to cool naturally for at least 30–40 minutes. — Carefully strain the oil through a paper filter or muslin (cheesecloth), then pour into sterilised bottles. — Seal and store in the pantry for up to 6 months.

CHEF'S TIP

When you pour the hot oil over the chillies, it's best to do so in a well-ventilated room, under a strong extraction hood or exhaust fan, as the fumes can be quite overpowering.

Green sauce forever

MAKES 500 ML (17 FL OZ)

This is a great way to use up any spare herbs you may have lying around, especially the soft herbs such as parsley, chives, tarragon, basil and oregano. It's a beautiful, vibrant green sauce that makes you feel healthy just looking at it, and is great to fold through pasta, noodles or vegetables, as well as a side bonus to a grilled steak or lamb cutlet.

240 g (8½ oz) mixed fresh herbs, e.g. parsley, chives, tarragon, basil, oregano, leaves only

60 g (2 oz) spring onions (scallions)

47 g (1½ oz) tin Ortiz anchovies in oil, drained

1 tablespoon salted capers, rinsed

5 Sicilian green olives (Castelvetrano), pitted

2 tablespoons of olive brine from the jar of Sicilian olives

1 bird's eye chilli, chopped

zest of 1 lemon

juice of half lemon

freshly milled black pepper

200 ml (7 fl oz) olive oil

Lightly chop the herbs and spring onions (scallions) to break them up slightly, then set to one side. — In a blender, combine the anchovies, capers, olives, brine, chilli, lemon zest and lemon juice and blitz until smooth. — Add the chopped herbs and spring onions, then blend with the anchovy mix until green and well-combined. — Season to taste with black pepper, then pour into an airtight container, levelling the top of the sauce. — Pour some extra olive oil over the top to protect it from air, then cover with a lid and refrigerate until required.

Kabayaki sauce

MAKES 200 ML (7 FL OZ)

Kabayaki is a traditional style of preparing eel in Japan, dipping it into a sweetened soy sauce (also known as kabayaki) and cooking it over charcoal to create a rich, sticky, smoky glaze.

In Japan, restaurants specialise in certain foods, such as sushi, tempura and yakitori, and develop their own style of house sauce. In a kabayaki restaurant, the mother sauce is used every day, refreshed with new mirin and soy and intensified by the continuous dipping of the grilled eel. Some restaurant's sauces can be decades old, with deeply developed smoky barbecue flavours.

This sauce is similar to teriyaki, without the additional garlic and ginger, and in many ways I prefer it, even for grilled meats.

240 ml (8 fl oz) Japanese soy sauce

240 ml (8 fl oz) mirin

50 g (1¾ oz) light brown sugar

Combine the soy, mirin and sugar in a heavy-based saucepan and bring to a simmer. — Reduce the heat to the lowest setting and simmer gently until the sauce is viscous enough to coat the back of the spoon. — Pour into a container and leave to cool. — Seal with a lid and refrigerate for up to 3 months, or freeze.

CHEF'S TIP

Cover the top of the sauce with a little extra olive oil to stop the herbs from oxidising and turning brown. No need to use an amazing extra-virgin olive oil, just an everyday one will do.

CHEF'S TIP

The sugar content in this sauce means it's very easy for the mixture to burn, so be very careful. Use a tall-sided pot if possible, and don't wander off halfway through!

Korean-style chilli paste

MAKES 220 G (8 OZ)

Gochujang is the king of the fermented Korean chilli pastes, adding life and soul to any dish it touches. One day I discovered I had no gochujang in the pantry, so decided to make my own with what I had to hand. It's different to the original, in a good way, with a lilting note of sweetness. I use the lighter shiro miso, but you can use the saltier, darker red miso if you prefer.

120 ml (4 fl oz) water
2 tablespoons honey
2 tablespoons mirin
3 level tablespoons Korean red chilli flakes (gochugaru)
70 g (2½ oz) shiro miso paste or red miso paste
1 tablespoon soy sauce
1 tablespoon rice vinegar
¼ teaspoon salt

Combine the water, honey and mirin in a saucepan and bring to a simmer, stirring until the honey dissolves. — Add the chilli flakes and miso paste, stirring to incorporate, and simmer until the mixture begins to bubble. — Turn off the heat and leave for 20 minutes to cool, then stir in the soy, vinegar and salt. — Cool and store in an airtight container in the refrigerator.

Lemon olive oil

MAKES 250 ML (8½ FL OZ)

This lovely oil adds a touch of summer to salads and dressings, grilled meats and fish.

You can, of course, buy lemon-infused olive oils, made by cold-pressing the lemons with the olives, but they tend to be expensive (and if they're not expensive, they may well be chemically enhanced). You can achieve a great result at home by using a Microplane to zest the lemons, and by infusing the zest into olive oil at a low temperature over a few hours. The olive oil essentially becomes a vehicle for the essential oils in the lemon, and is permeated with their amazing aroma and flavour.

250 ml (8½ fl oz) extra-virgin olive oil
zest of 3 lemons

Heat the oven to 85°C (185°F). — Combine the olive oil and lemon zest in a small, lidded, ovenproof saucepan and heat over a low–medium heat until the temperature of the oil reaches around 75°C (165°F). — Cover and put in the oven for 3 hours, stirring occasionally. — Remove and leave to cool, covered. — When cool, strain into an airtight container, seal and refrigerate for up to 2 months.

Lime and rice-wine vinegar

MAKES 250 ML (8½ FL OZ)

This is the perfect dressing for oysters, and the original vinegar I used at Sepia.

Most oyster dressings are made with bold red-wine vinegars or chopped shallots and lemon, which I find too dominating for fresh, briny oysters. Here, the seasoned rice-wine vinegar is softened by both kombu and sugar, so it isn't too aggressive, and the citrus burst from the fresh lime complements the oyster instead of overpowering it.

I really should have bottled this and sold it years ago.

200 ml (7 fl oz) Seasoned rice-wine vinegar (Basics, page 224)
2 limes

Zest the limes and set aside the zest. — Halve the limes and juice them, then strain the juice and measure out 50 ml (1¾ fl oz). — Combine lime zest, lime juice and seasoned rice-wine vinegar, mixing well. — Refrigerate in an airtight container for up to 1 month.

Marinated bullhorn peppers

MAKES 5 PEPPERS

Making your own charred and marinated peppers comes with a great sense of satisfaction. Start with fire – char them on a barbecue to get some heat and smoke into them, and finish them with a blowtorch to get the requisite char, otherwise they may overcook and become too soft.

Alternatively, seek out the deeply roasted, vibrantly dark red Navarrico Piquillo Roasted Peppers from Navarra in northern Spain, which are fruity, lightly spicy and beautifully intense.

5 bullhorn (romano) peppers, or 3 large red capsicums (bell peppers)
250 ml (8½ fl oz) extra-virgin olive oil
30 g (1 oz) thyme (about ½ bunch), whole sprigs
1 garlic clove, sliced

Heat the barbecue on high for 10 minutes. — Once hot, grill the peppers on all sides until lightly charred. — If you don't have a barbecue, arrange the peppers on a wire rack over a gas flame and scorch on all sides. — When nicely charred but not yet soft, arrange the peppers on a rack set over a tray, and use a blowtorch to blister the skin until blackened all over. — Arrange in a bowl covered with plastic wrap, and leave to steam for 15 minutes. — Peel off the skin and remove the seeds and any white membrane inside, then drain on paper towel to remove excess moisture. — To make the marinade, pour the olive oil into a small heavy-based saucepan and heat over a medium heat to around 100°C (210°F). — Add the thyme leaves and garlic, and leave to infuse for 5 minutes. — Arrange the peppers in a plastic container and cover with the infused oil, moving the peppers around to ensure the oil gets between the layers and covers them completely. If not, just top up with a little oil. — Seal and refrigerate for up to 3 weeks.

CHEF'S TIP

If you have a cold smoker you can smoke the capsicums (bell peppers), peppers and chilli before processing, to give them a different dimension.

Miso marinade

MAKES 600 G (1 LB 5 OZ)

This marinade is famous in Japan as the secret behind the famous miso cod, in which the fatty fish is cured in miso for up to 7 days, then grilled over charcoal until deeply caramelised. But it can also be used as a glaze for meats and vegetables, with a similar end result that is at once sweet, savoury, complex and succulent.

Saikyo miso is a very delicate and sweet white miso from Kyoto, made from rice rather than soybeans. It's worth seeking out.

200 ml (7 fl oz) sake

200 ml (7 fl oz) mirin

400 g (14 oz) saikyo miso (sweetened white miso)

Pour the sake and mirin into a saucepan and bring to a simmer, being careful that the liquid doesn't flame up from the alcohol. — Reduce the liquid by half, to 200 ml (7 fl oz). — Cool the mix and then whisk through the miso paste. — Pour into a container and refrigerate for up to a month, or freeze for 12 months.

Mushroom stock

MAKES 3 LITRES (101 FL OZ)

The combination of fresh and dried mushrooms gives this stock a meaty flavour that is rich with umami, while soy sauce contributes to the deep, rich colour, and mirin leaves a lingering sweetness. This stock is super versatile, and can be used for everything from cooking rice (Mushroom nori rice, page 55), to risotto or pasta, soups and broths.

For a meat-free version, use vegetable stock instead of chicken stock – it works brilliantly.

2.5 litres (85 fl oz) water

3 tablespoons dried porcini mushrooms

2 kg (4 lb 6 oz) Swiss brown mushrooms, cleaned

1 litre (34 fl oz) Chicken stock (Basics, page 215) or use vegetable stock for a vegetarian option

250 ml (8½ fl oz) light soy sauce

100 ml (3½ fl oz) mirin

1 teaspoon sea salt

½ teaspoon ground white pepper

Soak the dried porcini in the water for 1 hour. — Whiz the Swiss brown mushrooms in a food processor, until you have a coarse texture. — In a 6 litre (202 fl oz) heavy-based pot, combine the Swiss browns, stock, soy sauce, mirin, salt and pepper. — Add the soaked porcini and water, and bring to the boil, skimming occasionally. — Simmer gently for around 40 minutes, then remove from the heat and leave to stand for 10 minutes. — Strain through a paper filter or muslin, and leave to cool completely. — Store in 1 litre (34 fl oz) airtight containers and freeze until required.

My fermented chilli

MAKES 750 G (1 LB 11 OZ)

This is something I created at my restaurant Sepia and depended on as a staple for many years. Every late summer and early autumn we would gather the best of the capsicums (bell peppers) and peppers and take the time to make it. During the fermentation process, the flavour and acidity of the chillies deepen and grow more complex, and the colour becomes richer. It's a labour of love, but well worth the effort.

250 g (9 oz/about 2 large) red capsicums (bell peppers)

250 g (9 oz/about 2 large) bullhorn (romano) peppers

250 g (9 oz/about 12) long red chillies

125 g (4½ oz/about 50) bird's eye chillies

50 g (1¾ oz/about 5) habanero chillies

125 g (4½ oz) garlic cloves, freshly peeled

250 ml (8½ fl oz) still water

2.7% salt (see method)

Cut all the capsicums and chillies in half and de-seed, removing all the white membrane as well. — In a food processer, pulse the capsicums, chillies and garlic together with 200 ml (7 fl oz) of the water. — To calculate how much salt you will need, weigh the mix and multiply the weight by 2.7%. — (Here is a rough calculation, yours may vary slightly: 1.15 kg mixture × 2.7% = 31.5 g salt, or 2½ lb × 2.7% = 1.08 oz.) — Mix the salt into the remaining 50 ml (1¾ fl oz) water until dissolved, then add to the blended mixture, stirring well. — Pour into a mason jar and cover with muslin cloth, using an elastic band to hold the muslin in place. — Ferment for 3–4 days at room temperature, then transfer to sterilised jars, seal, and store in the refrigerator to ferment for a further 2 weeks. — To turn it into a paste, strain the mixture over a bowl and press out all the liquid. — Pour the liquid into a pan and simmer until the volume is reduced by half. — Combine the reduced chilli liquid and the strained chilli mixture in a blender and blend for 2 minutes, or until you have a fine paste. — Return the chilli paste to the pan and simmer for around 3-5 minutes, stirring continuously. — Remove from the heat and pour into a sterilised container. — Allow to cool completely, then cover and refrigerate for up to 1 month, or freeze for up to 1 year.

Pickled red onions for everything

SERVES 6

This is another great condiment that delivers a surprise hit of flavour and can really change the dimension of a dish. Pickled red onions help cut the richness of fatty dishes and really refresh the palate. We love them with everything from a mid-week burger to fancy grilled meats and rich salmon dishes, and always have them on hand. That's why I've called them pickled red onions 'for everything'!

2 red onions, peeled

160 ml (5½ fl oz) Seasoned rice-wine vinegar (Basics, page 224)

Cut the onions in half and then cut off the root on the angle so that the onion cells will separate. — Using a mandoline, finely slice the onions into a bowl. — Separate all the slices and individual cells with your fingers. — Pour the vinegar and 75 ml (2½ fl oz) water into a small pan and bring to a simmer. — Pour the mixture over the onions, pressing them down so they are covered in the vinegar. — Place a sheet of baking paper over the onions and then cover with a lid and cool in the refrigerator overnight. — Store in the refrigerator for up to 1 month. — To serve, use tongs to pick the onion from the vinegar, drain and serve in a bowl.

Ponzu sauce

MAKES 360 ML (12 FL OZ)

It might look like soy sauce, but ponzu has a tart, tangy, citrussy flavour with a light sweetness. This sauce is so versatile – it can be used as a dressing or a dipping sauce for seafood, cooked meats like shabu shabu, dumplings or tempura. This is a simplified version of the traditional Japanese condiment, because I want everyone to love it and use it as much as I do.

zest of 2 lemons, microplaned

130 ml (4½ fl oz) lemon juice, weighed after straining

65 ml (2¼ fl oz) Seasoned rice-wine vinegar (Basics, page 224)

100 g (3½ oz) caster (superfine) sugar

30 ml (1 fl oz) mirin

100 ml (3½ fl oz) white soy sauce

20 ml (¾ fl oz) light Japanese soy sauce

Mix the lemon zest and juice with the vinegar and sugar and stir until dissolved. — Add the mirin, white soy and soy sauce, stirring. — Store in an airtight container in the refrigerator for up to 1 month.

Rendered beef fat

MAKES 1 KG (2 LB 3 OZ)

For a chef, having a ready supply of fat is like having money in the bank, ready to draw on. And if we can use the fat that we trim from meat, we're not wasting anything. So I came up with the idea of rendering the fat with herbs and spices into a caramelised liquid, and sometimes even smoking the fat prior to rendering for even more flavour.

If you're worried about cooking with fat, just remember: fat is flavour, and the more flavour it has, the less you have to use.

2.5 kg (5½ lb) beef fat

100 ml (3½ fl oz) water

30 g (1 oz/about ½ bunch) lemon thyme, whole sprigs

1 tablespoon black peppercorns

Cut the fat into easy-to-handle pieces and put into a large bowl. — Rinse under cold running water to remove any blood, then drain. — Put the fat into a heavy based saucepan, then add the water and bring to a quick boil. — Reduce the heat to low–medium, and cook gently for about 1 hour or until the fat renders (melts). — Add the thyme and peppercorns, raise the heat a little and simmer until the fat turns golden brown. — Once caramelised, allow to cool, then strain through a filter or fine sieve into a 1 litre (34 fl oz) airtight container. — Refrigerate for up to 3 months, or freeze.

Roasted chicken fat

MAKES 300 G (10½ OZ)

I never waste anything! It is our responsibility as cooks to always respect what we are given, whether plant or animal.

I always buy whole chickens, and break them down into sections, saving everything from the bones and the neck to the skin and the fat – and I always put it to good use. With chicken on weekly rotation in our household, I like to save any excess chicken skin and fat and reserve it in the freezer for special occasions.

For this very special recipe, you'll need to save at least 1 kilogram (2 lb 3 oz) of skins and fat, over time. Add different spices and herbs to help make it your own, and be sure to really roast the skins in the pan as the fat renders, letting them caramelise until they are super toasty, to get that rich, deep golden colour.

1 kg (2 lb 3 oz) chicken skins and fat

150 ml (5 fl oz) cold water

1 teaspoon black peppercorns

30 g (1 oz/about ½ bunch) lemon thyme, whole sprigs

5 g salt

Wash the chicken skins under cold running water, and drain. — Put in a heavy-based saucepan and add the cold water. — Bring to a simmer and then turn the heat to low and simmer gently, stirring occasionally. As the water evaporates, the fat will start to render, and the skin will stick to the bottom of the pan. — Use a wooden spoon to scrape the base of the pan, allowing the skin to fry and caramelise in its own fat. — Add in the peppercorns, thyme and salt. — Keep the pan on the lowest setting as the fats start to brown. When it starts to smell as good as a roast chicken, it's nearly done – be careful not to take it too far. — Remove from the heat and carefully strain the fat into a heatproof container, pressing as much fat out as possible. — Discard the skins. — Allow the fat to cool, then pour into an airtight container, seal and freeze until required.

THE DINNER PARTY

Roasted garlic butter

MAKES 340 G (12 OZ)

Having garlic butter in the freezer is a godsend. I suggest you make more of this than the recipe states, so you can freeze it, either in an airtight container, or rolled into a sausage shape in plastic wrap, and then in kitchen foil. Once frozen, you can just slice off rounds to use when sautéing mushrooms, or serving on top of a just-grilled steak, rather than having to soften the entire amount. Using roasted garlic puree gives a more rounded and less aggressive garlic taste than raw garlic, and allows you to puree it until it is super smooth.

250 g (9 oz) unsalted butter, softened
80 g (2¾ oz) Roasted garlic puree (below)
20 g (¾ oz) parsley, chopped
1 teaspoon salt
cracked black pepper, to taste

In a bowl, mix the butter with a spatula until smooth. — Add the garlic puree, parsley, salt and pepper, and mix with the spatula until smooth. — Use immediately, freeze for future use, or transfer to an airtight container and refrigerate for up to 3 weeks. — Remove from the refrigerator a couple of hours before using.

CHEF TIP

To prep ahead, pick your herbs the day before and leave in a container lined above and below with damp paper towel.

Roasted garlic puree

MAKES 80 G (2¾ OZ)

For something that gives such a great result, this really couldn't be simpler. Sealing the garlic heads in kitchen foil means they roast as well as steam, in a technique similar to the French *en papillote*. Within the sealed pouch, internal pressure is created, and moisture turns into steam; a very gentle and effective way of cooking that gives you a very rich, smooth, nutty puree.

2 large heads of garlic, around 200 g (7 oz)
50 ml (1¾ fl oz) olive oil
½ teaspoon salt

Heat the oven to 180°C (360°F). — Cut straight across the tops of the heads of garlic to expose the tips of the cloves. — Make two squares of double-layered aluminium foil, and place a head of garlic on each square, cut-side up. — Drizzle with the olive oil and sprinkle the salt over, then seal the foil around the garlic and place on a baking tray. — Roast for around 45–55 minutes, or until the garlic is soft. — Leave the garlic to cool in the foil, then squeeze the skin of the cloves to push out all the cooked puree. — Pass the garlic puree through a fine sieve to remove any skin. — Use this to make roasted garlic butter (Basics, page 223), or store, covered with a layer of olive oil, in a small container in the refrigerator.

Romesco sauce

MAKES 600 G (1 LB 5 OZ)

I've long had a love affair with Spain, and this traditional tomato-based sauce from Catalonia is something I absolutely adore, even if I have changed a few flavours to make it my own, more Australian version.

I've added sun-dried tomatoes marinated in olive oil because their sweetly intense umami flavour really adds a kick, and I have replaced (sacrilege!) the almonds with home-grown macadamias because of their beautifully rich, buttery texture.

This is a great condiment to have in the refrigerator and a natural partner to grilled meats, fish and grilled vegetables.

2 long red chillies
100 g (3½ oz) macadamia nuts
180 g (6½ oz) roasted piquillo peppers, e.g. Navarrico
225 g (8 oz) sun-dried tomatoes, drained of their oil
2 tablespoons sherry vinegar
1 garlic clove, finely chopped
1 teaspoon hot-smoked paprika, e.g. La Chinata
1 teaspoon Aleppo dried chilli flakes
160 ml (5½ fl oz) olive oil

Place the long red chillies on a wire rack and set a heatproof tray underneath. — Using a blowtorch, char the chillies all over, until blackened. — Once charred, put into a bowl, cover with plastic wrap and allow to steam for around 15 minutes. — Using a knife, scrape off the charred skin, then cut open the chillies and remove the seeds and any white membrane. — Rest on paper towel to remove any excess moisture. — To prepare the macadamias, heat the oven to 130°C (265°F). Arrange the nuts on a tray and lightly spray with vegetable oil. Roast for 8–10 minutes, or until lightly golden in colour, giving the tray a shake halfway through the cooking to move the nuts around and ensure they cook evenly. — Transfer to a bowl and leave to cool. — Once cold, chop the nuts into quarters. — Pat dry the piquillo peppers and sun-dried tomatoes to remove any excess oil. — In a food processor, combine the charred chillies, piquillo peppers, sun-dried tomatoes, vinegar, garlic, paprika and chilli flakes, and blend lightly, to break up and combine. — Add the roasted macadamias and pulse to form a lumpy texture. — With the motor running, drizzle in the olive oil, then season with salt and pepper. — Transfer to an airtight container and refrigerate for up to 2 weeks.

Salmoriglio

MAKES 350 ML (12 FL OZ)

This is my little bit of zesty magic! Salmoriglio is basically a lemon and garlic dressing from southern Italy, with the addition of freshly chopped oregano and mint, and gives a bright, clean freshness to any fried or grilled fish, and to vegetables such as grilled eggplant (aubergine). Use this for a marinade or as a dressing. You can make the base dressing earlier in the day and leave it at room temperature, but be sure to blend in the herbs just before you serve, to keep them bright green. It would mute the freshness of the herbs if you added them any earlier.

20 g (¾ oz) fresh oregano leaves, picked
25 g (1 oz) fresh mint leaves, picked
1 garlic clove
2 lemons, zested
100 ml (3½ fl oz) lemon juice, strained (about 2 lemons)
1 teaspoon sea salt
1 teaspoon Aleppo chilli flakes
250 ml (8½ fl oz) olive oil

Combine the picked oregano and mint in an airtight container and refrigerate until required. — Crush the garlic and put in a jug with the lemon zest and juice, sea salt and chilli flakes. — Using a hand-held blender, blitz until smooth. — Gradually pour in the olive oil while blitzing, until all ingredients are well combined. — Set aside until ready to serve. — To serve, lightly chop the oregano and mint leaves, add to the blitzed mixture and blitz again until well-combined; you should be able to see flecks of herbs and chilli through the mix. — Serve at room temperature.

Saucy romesco

MAKES 320 G (11½ OZ)

A great sauce can play out in many different ways. Take romesco, for instance. If you combine it with hot-smoked paprika oil and then just add yoghurt, you'll have a super-spicy sauce with a freshness, creaminess and a smooth rounded palate that will complement everything on the plate. You can have all this ready to go, but always chop your herbs at the last minute to keep them fresh and protect them from oxidising.

200 g (7 oz) Romesco sauce (Basics, page 223)
100 g (3½ oz) Greek yoghurt
1 tablespoon Hot smoked paprika oil (Basics, page 226), plus extra to serve
20 g (¾ oz/about 1 small bunch), mint leaves, picked

In a bowl, mix together the romesco and yoghurt until well combined. — Fold through the paprika oil. — Pour into an airtight container and refrigerate until required. — Just before serving, chop the mint and fold through. — Spoon the romesco into a serving bowl and drizzle with extra paprika oil to finish. — Serve immediately.

Seasoned rice-wine vinegar

MAKES 1.9 LITRES (64 FL OZ)

If you have ever heard of 'awasezu', then this is it, and it's one of my favourite pantry staples. Japanese chefs use it primarily to season sushi rice, but it also works well for dressings, marinades, pickles and as a dipping sauce.

Kombu is Japanese dried kelp, available from Japanese and Asian grocers, and helps enrich and balance the vinegar. By storing the vinegar in the pantry with the kombu inside, it will continue to develop and soften over time – but if you can't find any kombu, it's fine to leave it out.

1.5 litres (51 fl oz) rice-wine vinegar
3 tablespoons sea salt
450 g (1 lb) caster (superfine) sugar
10 cm (4 in) stick of kombu (optional)

Combine all the ingredients in a large container with a lid, whisking to help dissolve the salt and sugar. — Cover and leave for a couple of days, stirring every so often. — Transfer into a bottle (along with the kombu, if using) and seal with a tight-fitting lid. — Store in the pantry until required.

CHEF TIP

To prep ahead, pick your herbs the day before, and leave in a container lined above and below with damp paper towel.

Shellfish oil

MAKES 1.1 LITRES (37 FL OZ)

For me, wasting food is wasting flavour, and flavour is something that is packed into the shells of all crustaceans. Every time I buy prawns (shrimp), scampi or lobster and don't use the heads or shells, I freeze them in a container so that I can make this oil.

This is great not only for pasta and noodles, but also for dressings and sauces, and it's the perfect finishing touch for grilled prawns or lobster straight off the barbecue. You might make it for a special dinner party, but I bet you end up using it for quick family meals on the run as well, just like I do.

150 ml (5 fl oz) grapeseed oil, for frying

1.6 kg (3½ lb) lobster shells or prawn (shrimp) shells

1 brown onion, chopped

1 small bulb of fennel, chopped

6 garlic cloves, crushed

1 bunch French tarragon

2 bay leaves

30 g (1 oz) thyme (about ½ bunch), whole sprigs

1 teaspoon black peppercorns, crushed

1 teaspoon fennel seeds

1 star anise

650 g (1 lb 7 oz) tomato paste, double concentrated (concentrated puree), e.g. Mutti

1 litre (34 fl oz) water

1.6 litres (54 fl oz) grapeseed oil

Heat a tall, heavy-based pot that will take at least 6 litres (202 fl oz) over a medium–high heat, and pour in the first amount (150 ml/5 fl oz) of grapeseed oil. — When the oil starts to smoke, add in one-third of the lobster or prawn shells and roast over a high heat until bright red and fragrant. — Add a further one-third of the shells and roast until they are bright red and producing a strong roasted shellfish aroma, then add the remaining one-third and continue to roast until bright red and fragrant. — Next, add the onion, fennel, garlic, tarragon, bay leaves, thyme, peppercorns, fennel seeds and star anise. — Reduce the heat to medium and continue to roast for a further 5 minutes, tossing occasionally, making sure the ingredients don't catch and burn. — Add the tomato paste and cook for a few minutes, tossing to coat everything in the pot. — Add the water and stir to combine as you bring the mixture to a simmer. — Slowly pour in the grapeseed oil, while stirring – it is the constant stirring that will help the oil and water emulsify and become viscous. — Turn the heat to low and cook for around 2–3 hours. From time to time, the oil will split from the water, so give it a big stir to keep them well mixed. The oil is ready when it is dark red in colour, fragrant and has separated and come to the surface of the pan. — Using a ladle, skim all the oil from the surface as best you can (it's okay to take some of the shellfish liquid at this stage) and set aside in a bowl. — Strain the remaining liquid and shells through another strainer, then discard the shells. — Pour the strained mixture back into the same cooking pot, bring to a simmer and then turn off the heat. This will allow more oil to split from the liquid, enabling you to skim more oil from the surface. — Add the newly skimmed oil to the first amount of oil. — Gently pour the oil into a clean pan, leaving any water that has settled at the bottom of the bowl. — Heat the oil over a low–medium heat. As it warms, the water will evaporate and the oil should become a clear, dark red (do not overheat at this stage). — Pass through a paper filter into a container and allow to cool. — When cool, either transfer to a bottle, seal and store in the refrigerator for up to 2 months, or freeze in airtight containers for up to 12 months.

CHEF'S TIP

If you have a 12 litre (405 fl oz) stockpot, then I suggest doubling this recipe, because I promise you are going to love this oil. Making things in bulk is not only more economical, it intensifies the flavour, too.

Smoked paprika oil (sweet or hot)

MAKES 450 ML (15 FL OZ)

Flavoured oils are a favourite of chefs all over the world (and very on-trend), and this soft, smoky, rich, dark red oil is a magnificent pantry item that will drip finesse over any dinner party.

Depending on the end use, I make this with either sweet smoked paprika, or hot smoked paprika. Both have a rich smokiness and vibrant red appeal, and I can never decide which one I like the most.

I particularly love the La Chinata brand of paprika from La Vera in the west of Spain, because it is made in the traditional style, smoked over oak. It's also fun to replace the smoked paprika with a good curry powder, harissa powder or espelette chilli powder; the possibilities are endless.

40 g (1½ oz) sweet smoked paprika
or hot smoked paprika

1 tablespoon garlic powder

1 teaspoon salt

500 ml (17 fl oz) grapeseed oil

Heat the oven to 75°C (165°F). — In a small, heavy-based saucepan, combine the paprika, garlic powder and salt, and mix. — Whisk in one-third of the grapeseed oil to make a thick paste. — Gradually pour in the remaining oil, whisking, until all the oil is incorporated. — Heat to around 65°C (150°F), while continuing to whisk. — Cover and transfer to the oven for 3–4 hours, stirring occasionally so all the ingredients are incorporated. — Strain the oil through a paper filter into a bottle, then seal and store in the pantry for up to 2 months.

Taberu rayu table chilli

MAKES 1.4 KG (3 LB 1 OZ)

Taberu rayu literally means 'chilli for eating', and is a Japanese table condiment usually eaten with noodles or rice. I have it with pretty much anything, however, because it's one of my favourite condiments, and you'll find it used in many recipes throughout this book.

It's relatively new to Japanese cuisine, which is always changing and evolving, and is thought to have originated in Okinawa around 2009, as an adaptation of China's style of chilli oil.

This is basically a chilli sesame oil to which I have added spring onions (scallions), garlic, ginger and paprika for extra oomph. I've also adapted this into a more textural version, crispy rayu chilli (Basics, page 215).

475 ml (16 fl oz) roasted sesame oil

200 g (7 oz) red onions, finely diced

50 g (1¾ oz) ginger, finely diced

50 g (1¾ oz) garlic, finely diced

2 bird's eye chillies, finely diced

100 g (3½ oz) spring onions (scallions), finely sliced

100 g (3½ oz) Korean chilli flakes (gochugaru hot)

40 g (1½ oz) sweet smoked paprika

2 level tablespoons shichimi togarashi

40 ml (1¼ fl oz) mirin

40 ml (1¼ fl oz) light soy sauce

2 tablespoons shio kombu (optional)

2 level tablespoons sugar

2 level tablespoons salt

4 tablespoons (40 g/1½ oz) white sesame seeds

2 tablespoons (20 g/¾ oz) black sesame seeds

600 ml (20½ fl oz) grapeseed oil

Heat the sesame oil in a large, heavy-based saucepan over a medium–high heat. — Add the red onions, ginger, garlic and bird's eye chilli and fry, without colouring, for around 4–5 minutes. — Add the spring onions and fry until soft and transparent. — Add the chilli flakes, smoked paprika and shichimi togarashi and cook until the mixture is deep red and becoming more of a paste. — Add the mirin and soy, and cook, stirring, until the liquid has evaporated. — Lower the heat and cook for a few minutes, then add the kombu (if using), sugar, salt and sesame seeds, and stir through. — Add the grapeseed oil and heat until the mixture begins to bubble, and the oil turns a rich red colour. — Turn off the heat and allow to cool naturally. — Once cold, refrigerate in an airtight container until required, for up to 2 months.

Toasted garlic oil

MAKES 300 ML (10 FL OZ)

Garlic is an amazing ingredient and appears in lot of my recipes, whether it's grated raw into dressings, slow-cooked in braises or roasted for butter, so why not turn it into an oil as well?

For this recipe you need to toast the garlic quite precisely, otherwise it will taste burnt and bitter, so take care, and remember that the garlic will continue to toast in the oil after you have removed it from the heat. Choose a cool bottle to store it in, so it looks good on the table, because this oil deserves to be out there on show, along with your food.

300 ml (10 fl oz) olive oil
4 large garlic cloves, skinned

Finely slice the garlic cloves (this is best done using a mandoline). — Pour the olive oil into a small, wide-based saucepan, then add the garlic. Use a fork to help separate the slices. — Place over a medium heat until the oil starts to bubble. — As the garlic slices start to fry, they will turn golden. Keep swirling them with the fork as they fry. — Be mindful of the colour of the garlic and the temperature of the oil, and remove from the heat as the garlic starts to brown and become crisp. — Pour immediately into a heatproof bowl. — Once cool, pour into a bottle and seal, and store in the pantry until required.

WHERE
TO
BUY

This is my little black book of some of the great producers, growers, importers, butchers and food specialists who have been a part of my life, both personally and professionally. It's their dedication and commitment to excellence that makes the difference between a simple dish and a special one.

I hope you seek them out, and enjoy the process of discovering new benchmarks of flavour. This is also my way of saying thank you to them, for their ongoing support of the hospitality industry and beyond.

OLSSON'S SALT

The Olsson family has been making solar sea salt since 1948, and is now the oldest family-owned and operated sea-salt producer in Australia. Alexandra Olsson has supplied my restaurant Sepia, and several other projects of mine, for many years, and I love all her salts, from sea salt and truffle salt to smoked salt, rubs, brines and other salt products. A true industry leader and supporter of hospitality.

OLSSONS.COM.AU

NIPPON FOOD

Motoi Hirasedo and his wife Victoria are the most amazing and knowledgeable people, dedicated to all things artisanal Japanese. Their online store includes the following amazing ingredients: Iwate soy sauce, Hon Mirin, Ishino Saikyo miso, rice vinegar and umeboshi. Do yourself a favour and check out their mind-bending array of sake as well. Wholesale only.

NIPPONFOOD.COM.AU (WHOLESALE ONLY)
JAPANESEPANTRY.COM.AU (RETAIL)
SAKEBOUTIQUE.COM.AU (RETAIL)

HERBIE'S SPICES

Ian and Liz Hemphill opened their shop in Rozelle 25 years ago, and have shared their wealth of knowledge with home cooks and chefs ever since. It's the one-stop spice shop, both in store and online.

HERBIES.COM.AU

BUTCHERS

VIC'S MEAT

Anthony Puharich and I met when I first arrived in Australia in 1996. We were two young guns, me as a chef and Anthony delivering meat for the family business, Vic's Meats, named after his father, Victor. Today, Anthony has grown the business to be Australia's premium wholesaler, with a beautiful boutique meat store known as Victor Churchill – the jewellery shop of butchers. Thank you for your incredible contribution to this book, and to Australia.

VICSMEAT.COM.AU
VICTORCHURCHILL.COM

SPECIALTY PRODUCTS

SIMON JOHNSON

Simon Johnson is an iconic Sydney retail store, founded by a man of the same name, that set the bar way back in the 1990s for quality ingredients from global artisans. Now part of a dynamic food group, along with Calendar Cheese Company, it's the largest distributor of specialty cheese and caviar in Australia. And an honourable mention goes to their Caviar Ambassador, Lisa Downs, who can source the finest caviars from sustainable producers across the globe for the ultimate luxury experience.

You'll see my favourite SJ products scattered throughout the recipes in this book: Navarrico Piquillo Roasted Pepper, La Chinta sweet and hot smoked paprika, Forvm vinegars (chardonnay, cabinet sauvignon and merlot), Tracklements condiments, Ortiz anchovies and Ortiz white anchovies (boquerones), and LeBlanc walnut and hazelnut oils. And for dessert, brutta e buoni biscotti, Valrhona Chocolate Manjari (64%), Dulcey Caramelised (35%), Blond Dulcey (32%), Milk Chocolate Valrhona Jivara (40%) and Valrhona Ivoire (35%).

SIMONJOHNSON.COM

OLIVE OILS

ALTO (NEW SOUTH WALES)

I use ALTO Pro Blend for dressings and general cooking, and ALTO Vividus and Robust for finishing dishes and for salads. Thank you to both Robert Armstrong and Westerly Isbaih for their ongoing efforts in bringing us Australia's finest olive oils and olives.

ALTO-OLIVES.COM.AU

JOSEPH (SOUTH AUSTRALIA)

Joe Grilli introduced us to his very first olive oil 27 years ago, and I've been hooked ever since. I use the iconic Joseph First Run and Cold Press for finishing dishes and for salads.

PRIMOESTATE.COM.AU

TRUFFLES

TRUFFLES OF AUSTRALIA

I have been involved with Australian truffles from the very beginning, when they were rare indeed, and I'm so proud of how Australia has grown to be one of the largest premium truffle-growing countries of the world. Leonie Poile of Truffles of Australia is dedicated to her task of showcasing Australian truffles on the international stage, and can source you the finest black gold from around the country and have it delivered directly to you.

INSTAGRAM: @TRUFFLESOFAUSTRALIA

SMALLGOODS

LP'S QUALITY MEATS

Luke Powell of LP's Quality Meats was a young chef who came into my kitchens at Tetsuya's 20 years ago. He has grown into a fine young chef and, by following his passion for charcuterie, into an equally fine producer of salami, sausages and other smallgoods.

LPSQUALITYMEATS.COM

SALUMI AUSTRALIA

I first met Massimo Scalas at the Noosa Food and Wine Festival in 2012, where I was blown away by the quality of his ethically farmed, cured and slow-aged meats. By the time I returned to Sydney, they were on the bar menu at Sepia. Based in the Northern Rivers of New South Wales, the company has since grown, and luckily his products are now available Australia-wide.

SALUMI.COM.AU

SEAFOOD

GETFISH

My dear friends Frank Theodore and Jason Craus of Getfish have been looking after me for the past 20 plus years. Knowing how particular I am with seafood, they are both relentless in their pursuit to source and deliver the best quality seafood there is. I would not be the chef I am today without their wealth and generosity of knowledge over the years.

Look out for these products in particular: Rockliff spanner crab, Yarra Valley trout roe, Hiramasa kingfish, Australian tiger, king, scarlet and banana prawns, lobsters, marron, Kinkawooka mussels and King George whiting.

GETFISH.COM.AU

CLEAN SEAS

Australia's premium supplier of the finest sashimi-grade kingfish. Ask for it by name, to be assured of the quality and freshness of this world-class fish.

CLEANSEAS.COM.AU/OUR-FISH

EQUIPMENT

These are two of the best places to buy kitchen equipment and specialised ingredients: Chefs' Warehouse, for wholesale, and The Essential Ingredient, for retail. Thank you both for your endeavours to supply everything we need to make our dinner party dreams possible.

CHEFSWAREHOUSE.COM.AU
ESSENTIALINGREDIENT.COM.AU

CHEESE

MAKER AND MONGER

I had heard a lot of great things about Anthony Femia and his wonderful Fromagerie at Prahran Market in Melbourne, and his was the first shop I visited when I moved to live in Melbourne. Anthony was so welcoming and hospitable, genuinely happy for me to be opening a restaurant in his hometown. His passion, intelligence and knowledge are second to none, not to mention his good humour. Make sure you visit his cheese shop, if only for one of his famous cheese toasties.

MAKERANDMONGER.COM.AU

THANK YOU

First of all, a big thank you to all those who have gathered at our table. We have held so many dinner parties over the years, and are blessed to have great friends who not only love food and wine, but most importantly, love great conversation and having fun!

Special thanks to this lot (not in any particular order, so don't start on me): Sue Elliott and Craig McGill, Sarah Jenkins, Bill Miller, Melissa Leong and Rob Mason, Stephen Bonnitcha and Leona Szeto, Ardyn Bernoth and Rob Thompson, Hayden Winch and Koren Wines, Garry Lyon and Nicky Brownless, Anthony and Rebecca Puharich, Annie Fitzpatrick and Peter Murphy, Dr Ken Loi and Shirley Guo, Dominic Rolfe and Amanda Hooton, Jon Osbeiston, Huon Hooke and of course our parents Lin and Ray Benn, Judith and Peter Wild.

The Dinner Party grew from a tiny seed planted in the middle of a dinner party, and has been nurtured by a great team of people into the beautiful book it is today. Some of the very special people we would like to thank:

Michael Harry of Hardie Grant, for the opportunity to bring the dinner party to life and inspire others to have as much fun as we do.

The magnificent Jill Dupleix for taking my words and making me sound more like myself. Smoothing off the rough edges and making sense of a chef's grammar, spelling and the sometimes dry, English wit hidden within the manuscript. Forever grateful.

Kristoffer Paulsen, photographer, for his eccentricity and brilliance. You get it.

Our wonderful stylist Jess Johnson, whose grace and style enhances absolutely everything.

And to the extraordinary designer Evi O, for your vision.

Jo Ward, the most talented pastry chef we have ever worked with, thank you for your time, skill and effort dedicated to working on this book.

Guillaume Verite, Australia's star sommelier of the future, for the wine style suggestions.

Our fabulous neighbours, who worked tirelessly to taste all the desserts as Martin was testing the recipes: Ralph and Rosemary Fitzgerald, Di Hines and family, and Martin Fuller and Vanessa Wegner.

Thank you to Woll Australia for supplying frypans from the Diamond Lite series for selected recipes, and to Maxwell & Williams for supplying the Caviar and Cashmere collections, used for recipe styling.

Of course, duCATi (sometimes known as Bubbles) our cat, who really does enjoy our dinner parties and guests as much as we do.

And to all my growers and suppliers over the years, a big thank you to you all, for making it such a pleasure to do what I do. In a wider sense, your passion, enthusiasm and dedication to excellence continues to shape our culinary landscape and should always be appreciated.

MARTIN BENN AND VICKI WILD

INDEX

Published in 2023 by Hardie Grant Books, an imprint of
Hardie Grant Publishing

Hardie Grant Books (Melbourne)
Wurundjeri Country
Building 1, 658 Church Street
Richmond, Victoria 3121

Hardie Grant Books (London)
5th & 6th Floors
52–54 Southwark Street
London SE1 1UN

hardiegrant.com/books

Hardie Grant acknowledges the Traditional Owners of the
Country on which we work, the Wurundjeri People of the
Kulin Nation and the Gadigal People of the Eora Nation, and
recognises their continuing connection to the land, waters
and culture. We pay our respects to their Elders past and
present.

The Dinner Party
ISBN 978 1 74379 896 6

10 9 8 7 6 5 4 3 2 1

Publisher: Michael Harry
Project Editor: Antonietta Anello
Editor: Vanessa Lanaway
Design Manager: Kristin Thomas
Designer: Evi-O.Studio | Evi O
Writer: Jill Dupleix
Photographer: Kristoffer Paulsen
Stylist: Jessica Johnson
Chef: Jo Ward
Production Manager: Todd Rechner
Production Coordinator: Jessica Harvie

Colour reproduction by Splitting Image Colour Studio

Printed in China by Leo Paper Products LTD.

A catalogue record for this
book is available from the
National Library of Australia